DINE OUT
AND
LOSE WEIGHT

By the same author:

EAT YOURSELF SLIM
THE MONTIGNAC METHOD – Just for Women
RECIPES AND MENUS
MONTIGNAC PROVENÇAL COOKBOOK
THE MIRACLE OF WINE

MONTIGNAC FOOD BOUTIQUES

United Kingdom:

160 Old Brompton Road LONDON SW5 0BA
Phone/Fax: 01 71 370 2010
http/www: global-m.com/montignac

France:

14 rue de Maubeuge 75009 PARIS
Phone: 01 49 95 93 42

5 rue Benjamin Franklin 75116 PARIS
Phone: 01 45 27 35 73

MICHEL MONTIGNAC

Preface by Leonardo Santi

DINE OUT
AND
LOSE WEIGHT

The French Guide to
Healthy Eating

*Translated from the original French version
"Comment maigrir en faisant des repas d'affaires"
and specially adapted for the UK.*

MONTIGNAC PUBLISHING UK

"Dine Out and Lose Weight"

Third Edition – Revised and Updated

First published in FRANCE under the title, *"Comment maigrir en faisant des repas d'affaires"*, 1987.

MONTIGNAC PUBLISHING UK LTD
1 LUMLEY STREET
LONDON W1Y 1TW

ISBN 2-906236-34-9

Filmset by Selwood Systems, Midsomer Norton
Printed and bound in Holland.
Production: GAC Bosmann, Velp.

Table of Contents

Table of Contents

Table of Contents

Note

The method described in this book is to be distinguished from the common "diet." It is a nutritional system based on the natural equilibrium of the body's metabolism.

If the method, which does not call for quantitative restrictions, is fully understood, no nutritional deficiencies should result. However, the method is designed, first and foremost, for a healthy subject, and if you are undergoing special treatment of any kind, you should check with a doctor before you apply the principles presented here.

In any case, it is highly recommended that everyone has a medical check-up before altering their diet, in order to be sure they are basically in good health and so as to be able to monitor the positive results that will follow.

About the Author

Michel Montignac has been in charge of personnel since the beginning of his professional career.

In 1981, he became Area Personnel Director for the European headquarters of an American pharmaceutical company.

In addition to his main responsibilities, he was regularly called upon to entertain the company's foreign visitors, and to dine in the best restaurants of the French capital.

Within three months, Montignac, who was already 13 pounds overweight, put on an extra 15 pounds. Moreover, obesity was not uncommon in his family.

He soon reached a point where he had difficulty in accepting his physical condition, and therefore decided to embark on an in-depth exploration of dietetic and nutritional phenomena. He began to study on his own – reading, interviewing experts, and conducting research in the scientific environment where he worked.

He met with doctors, physicians and researchers who were already familiar with the topic. He also conducted experiments on himself, his family and friends.

Within a few months, Montignac had lost 2 stone which, to this day, he has not put back on.

In 1987, he published his first book in France. Other titles followed and in the ensuing years his books have been translated into English, Spanish, German, Dutch and Finnish. Currently, over 5 million copies of his books have been sold in Europe alone.

Today, the principles presented in Montignac's book have been recognised by a significant majority within the French and the international medical establishment. A medical team that works closely with the author is currently training other doctors in the method.

About the Author

Montignac holds seminars especially designed for business professionals and he also runs courses for the increasing number of professional chefs who find the disciplines of the Montignac Method both a challenge and a stimulus to their creative abilities.

The author is 52 years old, married, and the father of three.

Preface

By Professor Leonardo Santi
"Dine Out and Lose Weight"

Certain readers might be surprised that the preface of a dietary book should be written by a doctor whose speciality is in an entirely different field.

The reason for this is not really all that surprising once one realises that diet plays an essential role in human health.

It is often forgotten that nutritional factors constitute the best prevention against even the most serious diseases. They are responsible for neutralising toxic agents, or at least preventing them from altering the cell's fundamental mechanisms.

It is well known, even among the general public, that an unbalanced diet constitutes the principal risk factor for most diseases. This is why it is important to correct bad eating habits and to adopt new, healthy ones, that provide the best safeguard against health problems.

When writing for the general public, it is always wise to ensure good comprehension of the technical dietary information. While stressing that it is in one's personal interest to change the bad eating habits that are ingrained in dietary habits, the information should, nevertheless, be conveyed in such a way as to avoid moralistic sermons and overly aggressive messages that could cause fear.

It would not be very reasonable to place the entire blame for an unhealthy diet on an individual's socio-cultural environment nor on the ways and customs of his region or country. Food, and the ritual that is attached to it, is not only one of the parameters of our modern day society, it is also one of the bases of our cultural heritage. This is why certain people are obliged, due to their social or economic status, to conduct their business affairs over lunches and dinners.

Businessmen and women should not have to be obsessed with the fear

Preface

that food will cause them to be overweight and/or lead them to have poor performance. This obsession will often lead to deprivation which can undermine one's professional effectiveness and general health. That is why, on behalf of all of those who like myself worry about the well-being of their contemporaries, I recommend Michel Montignac's book "Dine Out and Lose Weight" as a helpful aid in learning how to reconcile socio-professional obligations with the well-being of one's health.

Professor Leonardo Santi
*President of the International Society
for Preventative Oncology (I. S. P. 0.),
New York Scientific Director of the National
Institute for Cancer Research, Genoa, Italy*

Foreword

The principles of nutrition which I recommend in this book were originally intended for the French public, whose eating habits are quite different from those of a country like Britain.

I wrote this book for my compatriots to warn them that the more they abandon the culinary traditions of their country, the more they would suffer the secondary effects of bad diet, as is the case in English-speaking countries.

Such is the image of gastronomic delight which French cuisine inspires in the British imagination that the mere mention of it will make faces suddenly light up with pleasure.

But this initial reaction of pleasure is quickly followed by a more sceptical attitude, as the average person in this country is also convinced that by British standards, French cooking is far too rich.

In Paris, I once met a young American woman of 25 with the figure of a model. I asked her if she had always looked that way.

"No," she replied, "when I arrived in France I was 14 pounds overweight which I'd put on during my studies at the University."

"What did you do to lose them?"

"Nothing!" she told me. "I've been living with a traditional French family in Paris for a year and all I had to do to get rid of the extra kilos was to eat like the French."

On the other hand, I often get desperate calls from French parents whose children have spent a few months in the United States and who return with a worrying weight problem.

It should be noted that apart from Japan, France has the lowest average weight of all Western countries. Obesity is rare (about 4 times rarer than in the US), and when it does occur it is fairly limited. It is also rare for a French person to know his or her cholesterol level, as the rate of cardiovascular disease is very low in France (3–4 times lower than the US, according to the WHO). Only Japan does slightly better.

The reason for this is not genetic, but dietary habits.

Firstly, there is the nature of food itself. The French diet is more varied. The French eat more green vegetables, and therefore fibre. They do not eat sandwiches or hamburgers and, most importantly of all, they consume less sugar (77 lbs per person per year compared to 138 lbs in the U.S.). They drink wine (10 times more than in the U.S.), which has been proved to have exceptional nutritional qualities when taken in moderation. In particular, it protects against cardiovascular disease, which is definitely not the case with beer and soft drinks, where the reverse is true.

Secondly, the pattern of eating is different in France. French people eat 3 meals a day and do not snack in between. Lunch is a full meal over which time is spent, and a full meal consists of a starter, a main course and a dessert – usually cheese. In French schools there is always a cafeteria which serves a normal meal; the ritual of a jam sandwich and crisps in a lunch box, does not exist. At the workplace there is a proper lunch break and the food provided is not only varied but is usually freshly cooked at the last moment.

Then, every evening, the whole family gathers for dinner around the same table to share a meal which again, includes a starter, a main dish and a dessert.

Also much of the food is prepared in the home. Contrary to general belief, it only takes a few seconds to make "French" dressing, mayonnaise or tomato sauce.

Butter, charcuterie, oil, foie gras, fresh cream, cheese and wine are all part of the French daily diet and yet the French suffer from neither obesity nor heart disease.

Many American observers, journalists in particular, are beginning to take note and question the medical experts.

After all, why should we continue to restrict people's calorie intake, to remove cholesterol and fat from their food and to exhaust them with physical exercise, to achieve only poor results, or worse?

Would it not be wiser first to try to understand why the situation is better in France, where pleasure and gastronomy dominate everyday nutrition?

I believe this book partially answers these questions.

I wrote this book originally for the French, so they could be made aware of the risks they run in letting themselves be seduced by the American example of fast food and soft drinks, and of the advantage of conserving traditional French nutritional habits.

At the same time, it may show others the real reasons why they may themselves have reached crisis point with regard to their eating habits.

If people wish to achieve long-lasting results, which is easy if the recommendations found in this book are followed, they should accept two principles:

First, they should realise that it is the disorganised way in which they eat, rather than the quantity they may eat, which is at the root of their weight problem. They should also recognise that all sauce, mayonnaise and other pre-packaged foods constitute "polluted" foods, if only because of the astronomic amounts of sugar, starch and preservatives they contain.

They should then agree to change their eating habits. Frequent nibbling at pre-packaged meals and sandwiches should cease.

New habits, such as respect for lunch time and the systematic checking of food labels to identify undesirable ingredients, should be developed.

Experience has shown that the principles of nutrition contained in this book are quite compatible with the British way of life.

During my stays in Britain, I have personally verified that all restaurants and even fast food chains and coffee shops, include on their menus a possible choice of meal which would conform to the rules of the method we propose.

We have also checked that all the products and foods particularly recommended can be found in shops all over Britain.

The adoption of these principles of nutrition is therefore completely compatible with typical British family and professional life.

The only real effort to be made is a "gastronomic" one.

Michel Montignac

Introduction

I hesitated long before finally choosing the title of this book, "Dine Out and Lose Weight." At first, it seemed too commercial for a work that I had intended to be extremely serious. But in the end I stuck to this title to evoke the true purpose of the book rather than to impress my readers. After all, losing weight or not gaining it, is what you are really interested in!

Over the last few years, every time I was asked how I was able to lose weight and maintain that loss, I would answer that "I ate out and attended business meals." People smiled but were never fully convinced.

You too are also probably confused over this apparent paradox, especially if you blame your spare tyre on the professional obligations that call for you to indulge in "haute cuisine" a little too often. At any rate, this is what you have led yourself to believe.

Like most people, you have probably tried to apply those so-called "golden rules" of dieting and countless weight-loss methods which have by now become part of everyone's common knowledge. Nevertheless, you have noticed that the methods often contradict each other, and usually only produce temporary results, or even none at all. Moreover, you may have found it practically impossible to fit these diets into the framework of your professional lifestyle.

So today you are still in a frenzy over what we will discreetly call your "weight problem".

In the early 1980s, when I was well into my late thirties, my scales read 12 stone 8 pounds – about 13 pounds above my ideal weight. Nothing too alarming for a man over six feet tall and approaching his fortieth birthday.

Up to then I had led quite a conventional professional and social life, and my excess weight had apparently stabilised itself. I hardly ever overate, and when I did, it was usually in a family setting. When you come from the Southwest of France as I do, gastronomy is inevitably part of your heritage, culture and education.

I had already given up sugar, at least the dose I put in my coffee. I never ate potatoes, under the pretext that I was "allergic." And I hardly ever drank any alcohol, except for wine of course.

I had put on those extra 13 pounds over a ten year period – quite a moderate and progressive gain. When I looked around to gauge my portliness, I never felt above the norm, and in general I was in better shape than the average middle-aged man.

Overnight however, my professional lifestyle changed. I was transferred to the general headquarters of the American multinational company where I worked, and was suddenly given international responsibilities.

I spent much of my time travelling to visit the branches in my territory. These business trips were always punctuated with a series of business lunches and dinners.

In Paris, since I was in charge of internal public relations, it was my duty to accompany mostly foreign visitors to the best restaurants of the French capital. I must admit that this was not the most unpleasant part of my job, for I remain convinced that restaurants, meals, the dinner table – all pleasures aside – are the best place for discussion and communication. As a specialist in Human Relations, I can assure you that, for me, the best place for conducting negotiations (whether they be with the company chairman or with a new recruit) has always been in a restaurant setting, at the coffee shop across the street or even in the company cafeteria downstairs.

Three months after I was promoted to my new position however, I had already put on a few more pounds and weighed no less than 2 stone above my ideal weight. It must be added that during this period, I went to England for three weeks, which did little to remedy the situation.

The alarm bells were ringing. It was becoming a matter of urgency to do something.

Like everybody else, I had tried the usual weight-loss methods, which as we all know, never produce the hoped-for results.

But very soon thereafter, as chance would have it, I met a general practitioner with a keen interest in nutritional problems. He gave me some advice based on principles which seemed to question the foundations of traditional dietetics.

I quickly obtained some promising results and decided to look into the matter more thoroughly. Since I worked for a pharmaceutical company, it was relatively easy for me to gain access to the scientific information I needed.

A few weeks later, I had collected together most of the French and American publications on the topic. Even if the application of certain rules evidently brought results, I still wanted to understand the scientific bases underlying them. I wanted to know how the rules caused me to lose weight and what their limits were.

From the start, I told myself that I would not eliminate anything from my regular diet except for sugar, which I had been doing for a long time. When it is your mission to accompany visitors to restaurants to "entertain" them, it is simply out of the question to count calories and limit oneself to "a hard boiled egg and an apple". I needed to find another solution.

I therefore lost my 2 stone taking my business guests out for a meal at least once a day. Later on you will come to know and understand how this came about, but for the moment, let us just say that as one of the fundamentals of the method is based on the careful choice of dishes, a restaurant is quite evidently the ideal place to put it to the test.

However, the identifying of principles is one thing – applying them is something else.

After a few months, my friends and colleagues asked me to explain my "secret" to them. I therefore summarised the essential principles of my new weight-loss solution on three typewritten pages.

I tried, whenever possible, to spend at least one hour with each interested person, explaining the scientific basis for the method. But my subjects were inevitably influenced by false preconceptions on how to lose weight and these were frequently at odds with my method. As a result, they often quite involuntarily made blatant mistakes which compromised the results. A more complete explanation thus became imperative.

This book is a guide in which I have worked towards the following objectives:

– to help the reader shed certain preconceived ideas by reasoned argument
– to give the scientific foundations indispensable for a full understanding of nutritional phenomena
– to present simple rules and support them with basic scientific and technical explanations
– to make this a practical guide that the reader can always use as a reference.

With professional guidance, over the last few years I have observed, researched, tested and experimented. I am now thoroughly convinced that I have discovered and established a simple and efficient method to put into practice.

You will learn, as you read on, that "one does not put on weight by eating too much, but by eating badly."

You will learn to manage your diet, just as you manage your budget.

You will learn to reconcile your professional obligations with personal pleasure.

You will learn to improve your eating habits without taking the spice out of your meals.

This book is not a "Diet Book." Rather, it is an introduction to a new way of eating which will allow you to maintain your weight whilst you continue to enjoy your food.

In addition, you will be surprised to find that once you adopt this new way of eating, you will rediscover a long-lost feeling of physical and mental well-being.

You will learn that certain eating habits are often at the root of a lack of dynamism and, consequently, of physical or professional under-achievement.

You will also learn that by adopting certain fundamental nutritional principles which are easy to apply, you will eliminate the bouts of fatigue you have probably experienced in the past and you will rediscover an optimum vitality.

For these reasons, although your excess weight may be only modest or even non-existent, it is still important that you understand the principles to adopt for the proper management of your diet. This method is a passport to discovering new energy for you and your company, and guarantees improved professional efficiency.

You will also notice that any gastro-intestinal problems you may have had, will disappear for ever because your digestive system will establish a new equilibrium.

Although I may defend good French cuisine, especially wine and chocolate, I do not intend to trespass upon the excellent gastronomic guides I am sure you have on your shelves. I admit however, that I am often tempted to do so, since it is very difficult for me to disassociate nourishment from pleasure and simple cooking from gastronomic cuisine.

For some years now, I have been lucky to have visited some of the world's finest restaurants and for me, the handshake of a great chef is as much an inspiration as a benediction from the Pope. For great cuisine – often at its best when it is at its most simple – has truly become an art that I personally, would place before all others.

PART ONE

The Diet Scenario

1

What is the Solution?

Every year, after your annual medical check-up, you go home a little bit more desperate. Once again, you have put on weight since last year and although you had suspected as much, you do not want to admit it.

When you look at yourself in the bathroom mirror, you automatically pull in your stomach as if you were trying to impress someone on the beach. Close your eyes and hopefully the problem will go away.

It is not easy to admit that this is one area in life where you can never win. And it is all the more difficult to accept that fact when you are by nature a "winner", someone who never shies away from a challenge.

Over the years, you may have fought with your boss or with members of the board. You fought to move up, to get a promotion, to realise your goals and maybe even your dreams. You fought to become the person you are today.

You know how to solve problems, find efficient solutions, make decisions, lead and organise. You may even be a model of inspiration for your colleagues at work.

But when the doctor says "you have put on weight again!," you want to crawl under the table, ashamed and embarrassed.

And like a child who has not done his homework, you desperately try to find an excuse.

"But doctor, I don't understand," you manage to splutter. "I watch what I eat and I try not to eat too much. It's true. I can assure you that I eat much less than I used to. Of course, you understand, I cannot avoid business meals. They are a part of my job. But I am being extra careful. I even exercise. I have started jogging and I run for miles every week. But when I see the results, it isn't very encouraging. Maybe it's the all-too-frequent change in foods; you know, today New York, tomorrow Paris, and Hong-Kong the day after. Maybe it's jet-lag. ... No, it's

3

true. I've noticed that jet-lag makes me bloated. .... And if you saw what they are serving on planes nowadays... It's rubbish!"

Your doctor begins to smile. He has heard it all before.

"Well," he says as he gets up from his chair, "you must be careful or the situation could become dangerous. An active person such as yourself, under constant stress at work, is already a prime candidate for heart disease. So don't make it any worse for yourself by adding fat to your problems."

"Then doctor, tell me what I should do!"

"Eat less, drink less, and exercise! Start a diet!"

A diet! You have tried everything. Your extra weight is enough of a problem by now to ensure you know a great deal about diets already. Your spouse, your friends, even your secretary at work, talk enough about this subject for you to have become almost an expert in the field.

How many times have you stumbled upon a magazine article that promised quick weight loss?

You have learned to chew well, to rule out bread, not to drink while you eat, to have meals consisting only of fruit, to avoid fats and of course, to count your calories. You are repeatedly told not to consume too many rich foods and to exercise. But you have tried all that. You have cut down on alcohol. You have bought a bike, and have even taken up jogging.

And what are the results? Absolutely none. ... You may have lost a few pounds, but you have quickly put them back on again.

So, since you are not the type to despair, following your medical check-up you try to cast from your soul any guilty feelings that may still persist.

You reassure yourself that the people around you accept you just the way you are. In other words, you have become something of a fatalist.

However, deep down inside you know you cannot accept permanent defeat in this battle. You win all your other battles and like your colleagues, you are always on the look-out for new information that could bring you the solution.

Well, I think I have found it.

In fact, I am sure I have found it!

I have experimented successfully with it on myself and on a large number of people around me. Now it is your turn to discover it and put it into practice with the same success.

I wish you well!

2

Food Classification

In my view, this is the only chapter which may prove difficult to grasp in view of its technical nature. If this is the case, please forgive me.

Throughout the rest of the book, I will be talking about categories of edible substances and it will be useful if you have a basic understanding of what they are, otherwise you may fail to grasp the principles of the method.

I have tried to reduce this chapter to its essentials and make it as clear as possible. Though some of the ground it covers may be new to you, no part should remain unclear and you should not hesitate to return regularly to this section of the book, to ensure that you have fully understood the novel concepts that it contains.

Foods are edible substances that contain a number of organic elements such as proteins, lipids, carbohydrates, minerals and vitamins, as well as water and non-digestible matter.

PROTEINS

Proteins are the organic cells that make up living matter: muscles, organs, the brain, the skeletal structure, etc. They are made up of simpler bodies called amino acids. Some amino acids are produced by the body, but for the most part, they are introduced into the system through different ingested foods. Protein comes from two sources:

- *Animal sources:* meats, fish, cheese, eggs and milk.
- *Vegetable sources:* soya beans, almonds, hazelnuts, peanuts and certain leguminous plants.

Foods from plant sources, except soya bean, generally contain a low quantity of protein. They therefore cannot meet our physiological needs on their own.

A diet low in protein, however, can lead to serious consequences: muscle deterioration, wrinkling of the skin and immune system deficiencies.

We need to consume about three ounces of protein a day. Protein is needed to produce blood corpuscles, secrete hormones, produce scar tissue and maintain muscle tone. If the amount of protein consumed is really too great when physical activity is low, unburned protein residues will remain in the body and be transformed into uric acid, which lead in particular to gout.

CARBOHYDRATES

Carbohydrates are molecules composed of carbon, oxygen and hydrogen.

Blood glucose level (Glycaemia)

Glucose is the body's principle "fuel." It is stored in the form of glycogen in the muscles and liver.

Glycaemia is the term used here for the level of glucose in the bloodstream. On an empty stomach, this glucose level is normally one gram per litre of blood. When carbohydrate (bread, honey, cereal, sweets, etc.) has been ingested on an empty stomach, the effect on the blood sugar level is found to be as follows:

– In the first phase, glycaemia rises (to a greater or lesser degree, according to the nature of the carbohydrate).

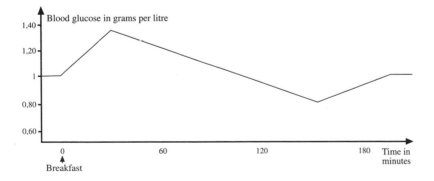

7

- In the second phase, following secretion of insulin from the pancreas, the blood glucose level falls and glucose is released into the tissues of the body.

- the third phase, the blood sugar level reverts to normal (see graph on previous page).

For many years, carbohydrates were placed into two distinct categories: "quick sugars" and "slow sugars", the terms referring to the body's rate of assimilating them.

"Quick sugars" were simple sugars, such as glucose, and disaccharides, found in refined sugars (both cane and beet), honey and fruit.

The term "quick sugar" owed its existence to the belief that, because of the simple nature of the molecule, these sugars were rapidly assimilated by the body after ingestion.

Conversely, "slow sugars" referred to all carbohydrates whose more complex molecule had first to be chemically transformed into simple sugar (glucose) in the course of digestion. This applied notably to the starches in cereals, from which it was thought that glucose was released into the body slowly and progressively.

This way of classifying carbohydrates is today completely outdated, and is based on a mistaken theory

Recent studies show that the complexity of the carbohydrate molecule does not actually determine the speed with which glucose is released to be absorbed into the body.

It is now accepted that the glycaemic peak (that is, the point of maximum glucose absorption), is reached at the same rate for any carbohydrate eaten in isolation and on an empty stomach, and occurs about half an hour after ingestion. So, instead of talking about the speed of assimilation, it is more to the point to consider the effect different carbohydrates have on the glycaemic level – that is, how much glucose they produce in the bloodstream after a given time.

It is therefore agreed by scientists and others in the field of nutrition (see bibliography), that carbohydrates should now be classified according to what is called their hyperglycaemic potential, as defined by the glycaemic index.

The Glycaemic Index

The potential of each carbohydrate to induce a rise in blood glucose (glycaemia) is defined by the glycaemic index, first used in 1976. This index is derived from the area below the glycaemic curve (shaded in the graph – see below) which is induced by ingestion of a particular carbohydrate.

Glucose is arbitrarily given an index of 100, standing for the area below its own glycaemic curve. The glycaemic index of other carbohydrates can then be arrived at using the following formula:

$$\frac{\text{area below curve of carbohydrate tested}}{\text{Area below curve of glucose}} \times 100$$

The higher the glycaemia induced by the carbohydrate in question, the higher will be its glycaemic index.

It should be noted that chemical processing of carbo-hydrates raises

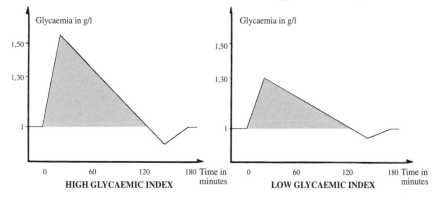

their glycaemic index. For example, cornflakes have a glycaemic index of 85, while maize in its natural state has an index of 70; instant potato has a glycaemic index of 95, whereas the index of boiled potatoes is 70.

The cooking of carbohydrates can have a similar effect. Carrots when cooked, have a glycaemic index of 90, whereas served raw they only have an index of 30.

In the interests of keeping things simple, I propose to place carbo-hydrates in one of two categories: "good carbohydrates" (with a low glycaemic index) and "bad carbohydrates" (with a high glycaemic index). This is the distinction which, as you will discover in the following chapters, will enable you to discover some of the reasons for being overweight.

Glycaemic Index Table

CARBOHYDRATES with high glycaemic index (bad carbohydrates)		CARBOHYDRATES with low glycaemic index (good carbohydrates)	
Maltose	110	Wholemeal bread or bread with bran	50
Glucose	100	Wholegrain rice	50
Fried potatoes	95	Peas	50
Very white bread	95	Wholegrain cereals without sugar	50
Mashed potatoes	95	Oat flakes	40
Honey	90	Fresh fruit juice (without sugar)	40
Carrots (cooked)	85	Wholemeal rye bread	40
Cornflakes, popcorn	85	Wholewheat pasta	40
Sugar (sucrose)	75	Red kidney beans	40
White bread	75	Dried peas	35
Refined cereals with sugar	70	100% stoneground wholemeal bread	35
Chocolate bars	70	Milk products	35
Boiled potatoes	70	Dried beans	30
Biscuits	70	Lentils	30
Corn (maize)	70	Chickpeas	30
White rice	70	100% stoneground wholewheat pasta	30
Brown bread	65	Fresh fruit	30
Beetroot	65	Carrots (raw)	30
Bananas	60	Fruit preserve (without sugar)	25
Dry fruit	60	Dark chocolate (over 60% cocoa)	22
Jam	55	Fructose	20
Non-wholewheat pasta	55	Soya	15
		Green vegetables, tomatoes, lemon, mushrooms	< 15

Bad Carbohydrates

These are all the carbohydrates whose absorption leads to a large rise in blood glucose.

This is what happens when table sugar is ingested in whatever form (on its own or combined with other foodstuffs, as in cakes). The classification also covers all processed carbohydrates, such as white flour and white rice, and alcohol (particularly spirits), as well as potatoes and maize.

Good Carbohydrates

Unlike the carbohydrates mentioned above, "good carbohydrates" are those which are only partly assimilated by the body, and which therefore produce a much smaller rise in blood glucose level.

They incolde whole cereals (unrefined flour, for example) whole rice and some starchy foods, such as lentlils and beans. Most importantly, they also include most of the fruits and vegetables which can also be classified as fibre (leeks, lettuce, green beans, etc.) and which all contain a small quantity of glucose.

LIPIDS (or FATS)

Lipids, or fats, have complex molecules. These are divided into two broad categories, according to their origin:

- *Lipids of animal origin*: these are found in meats, fish, butter, cheese, cream, etc.
- *Lipids of vegetable origin*: these are vegetable oils, margarine, etc.

They can also be divided into two categories of fatty acids:

- **Saturated fatty acids**, found in meat, cooked meats and pate's, eggs and dairy products (milk, butter, cheese, cream).
- **Unsaturated or Polyunsaturated fatty acids**: these are the fats that remain liquid at room temperature (sunflower oil, rapeseed oil, olive oil), though some can be solidified by hydrogenation (as in margarine manufacture). Included in this category are all fish oils.

Lipids are necessary in the diet. They contain a number of vitamins (A, D, E, K), as well as essential fatty acids (linoleic acid and linolenic acid), and they help in the synthesis of various hormones.

When lipids are mixed with bad carbohydrates, their assimilation by the body is interfered with and, as a result, fat reserves are laid down.

11

As a general rule, we eat too much fat. Lipids actually account for 42% of our energy intake, but it would be preferable if they did not exceed 30%. An excessive intake of lipids in conjunction with an excessive intake of some carbohydrates can lead to the development of cardiovascular disease.

Lipids are responsible for cholesterol, but in reality there exist two types of cholesterol, the "good" and the "bad". The aim is to keep the total cholesterol level as low as possible, with "good" cholesterol accounting for the greater part.

What needs to be understood is that not all lipids lead to an increase in "bad" cholesterol. In fact, there are certain ones which tend to lower the "bad" cholesterol level significantly.

To be totally precise, it is necessary to classify fats into three further categories:

1 *Fats which raise cholesterol*
  These are saturated fats found in meat, butter, cooked meats, cheese and lard.
2 *Fats which have very little effect on cholesterol*
  These are found in skinless poultry, shellfish and eggs.
3 *Fats which lower cholesterol and therefore help to prevent fat deposits*
  These include olive and corn oils, rapeseed oil and sunflower margarines.

As for fish oils (especially those of the oilier fish such as salmon, tuna, herrings, sardines, mackerel), these bring down the level of triglycerides and help prevent thromboses by "thinning" the blood. They are therefore useful in helping to prevent cardiovascular disease.

The weight-loss method which I advocate depends in part on choosing between "good" and "bad" carbohydrates. In the same way, choices have to be made between "good" and "bad" lipids, especially if you tend to have a high cholesterol level or simply want to guard against such an eventuality.[1]

---

[1] A complete chapter is dedicated to Hypercholesterolaemia as to its consequences with regard to cardio-vascular disease, See p. 187 in the Technical Appendix.

I would encourage you to refer to it to ensure that the food selections you make following the method, are the correct ones.

ALIMENTARY FIBRES

These are substances found mainly in vegetables, fruit and whole cereals.

Although it is true that they have no energy value, alimentary fibres play an extremely important role in the digestive process. The cellulose, lignin, pectin and the gums that they contain ensure good intestinal function, and their absence is the cause of most constipation. Moreover, these fibres are very rich in vitamins and trace elements[2], without which serious nutritional deficiencies can occur.

Some types of fibre activate the secretion of the bile salts which digest fats and regulate intestinal function. They also block the assimilation of fats, reducing the risk of atherosclerosis. In addition they lower the absorption of carbohydrates, thus limiting the rise in blood sugar levels (glycaemia)[3].

Fibre has yet another advantage. It limits the toxic effects of certain chemical substances, such as additives and colourings. And gastro-enterologists believe that some forms of fibre even protect the colon from a number of risks, particularly that of cancer.

In general, we have a daily dietary fibre intake below the recommended daily intake of 40 grams. A study done by the American CSFII in 1985–86, showed that in the United States women in the 20–49 year age group, received approximately 11 grams and children in the 1–5 year age group, received approximately 10 grams of dietary fibre per day. A report from the CSFII in 1985, indicated that on average, the dietary fibre intake of men was higher than that of women by about 17 grams per day[4].

Regarding the benefits to be derived from eating fibre, the experience of the Italians is given as an example.

Thirty years ago, the essentials of their diet were vegetables and wholewheat pasta – both of which contained high amounts of fibre. However today, due to the increase in the standard of living, meat figures more prominently in the national diet and pasta is made with processed flour. During the intervening period. the Italian medical authorities have

---

[2] Trace Elements: metals or metalloids present in infinitesimal quantities within the organism, necessary as catalysts for certain chemical reactions of the organism.
[3] See Technical Appendix p.181
[4] See 'Nutritional Monitoring in the United States: an Update Report on Nutrition Monitoring 1989' p.55.

noticed not only an increase in obesity but also of digestive cancers, which they have ascribed to the reduction in fibre intake.

FIBRE SOURCES AND THEIR CONCENTRATION (as a percentage of total weight)			
CEREAL PRODUCTS		**DRIED OILY FRUIT**	
Bran	40.0%	Dried Coconuts	24.3%
Wholemeal bread	13.0%	Dried figs	18.0%
White bread	1.0%	Almonds	14.3%
Wholemeal flour	9.0%	Raisins	7.1%
Whole rice	5.0%	Dates	9.0%
White rice	1.0%	Peanuts	8.0%
DRIED VEGETABLES		**GREEN VEGETABLES**	
Dried beans	25.3%	Green cooked peas	12.0%
Lentils	12.0%	Parsley	9.0%
Split peas	23.0%	Artichoke	4.0%
Chick peas	2.0%	Leeks	4.0%
		Cabbage	4.0%
FRESH FRUITS		Radishes	3.0%
Raspberries	8.0%	Mushrooms	2.5%
Pears with skin	3.0%	Carrots	2.0%
Apples with skin	3.0%	Lettuce	2.0%
Strawberries	2.0%	Cooked Spinach	7.0%
Peaches	2.0%	Lamb's lettuce	5.0%

It is now widely accepted that fibre has a beneficial effect in reducing obesity and its introduction into the diet tends to lower the levels of both glucose and insulin in the blood. Insulin secretions, as we shall discuss in the next chapter, are responsible for fat reserves.

Of the four main groups of nutrients, proteins are absolutely essential to our bodies, as they contain vital amino acids which we cannot make ourselves. Equally important are certain lipids, which contain essential fatty acids (linoleic acid and linolenic acid) that our cells are incapable of producing independently. Only carbohydrates may be considered

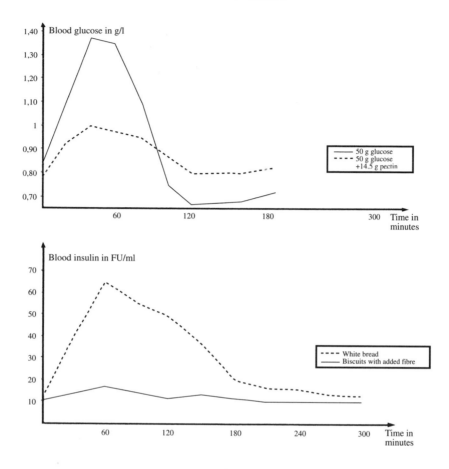

more expendable, since the human body is able to make its own glucose from stored fats (containing triglycerides)[5].

Lipids often occur in foods in conjunction either with protein, as in meat, or with carbohydrate, as in peanuts. Lipids and carbohydrates have a high energy rating and have therefore the potential of being stored in the body as fat. This is particularly the case when they are ingested together.

Proteins, on the other hand, have a low energy rating. Though essential for the well-being of our bodies, they have no bearing on the problems associated with high-energy foods.

That is why, for the sake of clarity, in this book we will leave aside

[5] See the Cycle of Krebs — Technical Appendix p.173

15

the category of proteins and whenever we mention a particular food, we will describe it only in terms of one of the following three divisions:

1. *carbohydrates* (specifying whether they are "good" or "bad")
2. *lipids*
3. *alimentary fibre*

When a food contains both carbohydrates and lipids, as in the case of peanuts, we will refer to it as a *carbohydrate-lipid*.

Summary

Proteins are substances contained in a number of foods of animal or vegetable origin. They are found in meat, fish, eggs and dairy products. Proteins are indispensable to the human body and their residual energy potential is very low.

Carbohydrates are substances that are metabolised into glucose. They are found in foods which originally contain either sugar (fruit, honey) or starch (flour, cereals, legumes). All carbohydrates on an empty stomach are absorbed at the same rate. They are classified according to their glycaemic potential, measured by the glycaemic index. It is therefore possible to draw a distinction between "good carbohydrates" with a low index and "bad carbohydrates" with a high index.

Lipids are substances of animal or vegetable origin. They are fats (meat, cooked meats, fish, butter, oil, cheeses, etc.). Some have the potential to raise blood cholesterol (meat, cheese), while others actually help to lower it (olive oil, etc.).

Alimentary fibre: in this category come all green vegetables (lettuce, chicory, leeks, spinach, green beans, etc.). Some dried vegetables, fruit and whole grains also contain a significant amount of fibre. It should be consumed frequently; failure to do so can lead to serious deficiencies.

Classification of Lipids, Carbohydrates, Carbohydrate-Lipids and Fibre

LIPIDS*	CARBOHYDRATES	CARBOHYDRATE-LIPIDS	FIBRE
Meat	Flour	Milk	Asparagus
– Lamb	Bread	Walnuts	Lettuce
– Beef	Rusks	Hazelnuts	Spinach
– Veal	Potatoes	Almonds	Tomatoes
– Pork	Rice	Peanuts	Aubergine
Poultry	Pasta	Liver	Courgette
Rabbit	Semolina	Soy Flour	Celery
Fish	Couscous	Wheat Germ	Cabbage
Crab	Tapioca	Egg Noodles	Cauliflower
Shrimp	Beans	Cashews	Sauerkraut
Prawns	Peas	Coconut	String Beans
Lobster	Lentils	Chocolate	Leeks
Eggs	Chick Peas	Olives	Artichokes
Cooked	Sugar	Chestnuts	Carrots
Meats	Honey	Water Cress	Peppers
Butter	Alcohol	Nuts	Endives
Cheeses	Sweetcorn	Scallops	Mushrooms
Olive Oil	Fruit	Oysters	Turnips
Margarine	Dried Fruit	Avocado	Salsify

* All foods in this column (except butter and oils) also contain protein.

Carbohydrate Classification

BAD CARBOHYDRATES	GOOD CARBOHYDRATES
Cane Sugar	Whole Cereals
Beet Sugar	(wheat, oats, barley, millet, etc.)
Brown Sugar	Wholemeal Flour
Honey	Wholemeal Bread
Maple Syrup	Bran
Sweets	Brown Rice
Molasses	Wholewheat Pasta
Jams, Jellies	Wheat Germ
Soft Drinks	Beans
Bleached Flour	Lentils
(French bread, rolls)	Chick peas
Cakes	Fruits (fresh and dried)
(made with white flour and sugar)	Chocolate
Pizza	(with more than 60% cocoa)
Biscuits, Croissants	Carrots (uncooked)
Quiche, Vol au Vent, Pies	

	EXCELLENT CARBOHYDRATES (LESS THAN 15 GLYCAEMIC INDEX)

BAD CARBOHYDRATES (cont.)		
Pasta	Alphalpha Sprouts	Mushrooms
(spaghetti, ravioli)	Broccoli	Cabbage
White Rice	Celery	Cauliflower
Potatoes	Turnips	String Beans
Sweet Potatoes	Soy Beans	Leeks
Potato Starch	Bamboo Shoots	Artichokes
Cornflour	Hearts of Palm	Peppers
Sweetcorn	Salsify	Lettuce
Carrots (cooked)	Aubergine	Spinach
Semolina, Couscous	Courgettes	Split Peas
Refined Cereals	Cucumbers	
– Corn flakes	Tomatoes	
– Puffed Rice	Radishes	
Alcohol		
(especially spirits)		
Chocolate		
(with less than 60% cocoa)		

3

The Calorie Myth

The calorie theory is probably the greatest "scientific swindle" of the twentieth century.

It is nothing more than a trap, a deception, a dangerously simplistic hypothesis, not based on any validated scientific data. And yet it has dictated our eating habits for over half a century.

Look around and you will see that the plump, the portly, even the obese, are precisely those who count their calories with the greatest religious fervour.

Everything that has been called a "diet" since the early thirties – with a few exceptions – has essentially been based on the low calorie approach.

How misguided can you be! No serious or lasting weight loss can ever be achieved through this method, not to mention the disastrous side-effects that can result.

At the end of this chapter, I will come back to the scarcely less scandalous "socio-cultural" effects of the calorie theory, that are a direct result of what can only be called "collective brainwashing."

ORIGINS OF THE CALORIE THEORY

In 1930 two American doctors from the University of Michigan, New-burgh and Johnston, suggested in one of their papers that "obesity results from a diet too high in calories, rather than from any metabolic deficiency".

Unfortunately, their study on energy balance was based on limited observations, and above all had been conducted over a period of time that was far too short to establish any serious conclusions.

But despite these weaknesses, the publication of their study received much acclaim and was immediately accepted as an irrefutable truth. Their word has since been considered gospel.

Several years later, however, Newburgh and Johnston, somewhat troubled by the public excitement over their discoveries, quietly published some serious reservations they had on their findings. These went entirely unnoticed. Their initial theory was already integrated into the syllabus of most Western medical schools, and there it remains to this day.

THE CALORIE THEORY

One calorie is equal to the amount of energy or heat needed to raise the temperature of one gram of water from 14° to 15° centigrade[1].

The human body needs energy; first and foremost, to maintain its body temperature at 98.6° Fahrenheit. When the body is active, additional energy is required to move, to speak, or simply to remain standing in a vertical position. On top of this, more energy is needed to eat, digest, and carry out the basic activities of daily life.

The daily energy requirements of the body vary with age and gender, and from one individual to another.

The calorie theory is as follows:

If an individual needs 2,500 calories a day and only consumes 2,000, a 500 calorie deficit results. To compensate for this deficit, the body will draw on its fat reserves to find an equivalent amount of energy, and weight loss will follow.

If, on the other hand, an individual regularly consumes 3,500 calories whereas 2,500 would suffice, the excess 1,000 calories will automatically be stored away in the form of fat.

The theory is therefore based on the assumption that there is never any loss of energy. The theory is purely mathematical, directly inspired by Lavoisier's theory on the laws of thermodynamics.

At this point, we may ask ourselves how prisoners in Nazi concentration camps survived for nearly five years on only 700 to 800 calories a day. If the calorie theory was indeed correct, the prisoners would have died

[1] See more on calories in the Technical Appendix p.199.

once their fat stocks were exhausted – in other words, within a few months.

Similarly, we can ask ourselves why hearty eaters who consume about 4,000 to 5,000 calories a day never grow fatter. In fact, some even remain skinny. If the theory held true, these hearty eaters would weigh over 70 stone after only a couple of years.

Moreover, how does one explain that certain people put on weight even though they restrict their diet and reduce their daily ration of calories? Ironically, this is how thousands of people put on more and more weight while starving themselves to death.

Statistics also show that more than 50% of the obese eat less than the average.

THE EXPLANATION

Why does weight loss fail to occur despite a reduction in one's calorie intake?

Actually, weight loss does occur, but only temporarily. The error of Doctors Newburgh and Johnston is that they conducted these observations over too short a period of time.

The phenomenon works like this

Let us imagine that an individual needs 2,500 calories a day and, over a period of time, consumes accordingly. If, suddenly, the ration of available calories falls to 2,000, the body will then use the equivalent amount in stored fat to compensate, and weight loss will result.

However, if the individual now continues to consume 2,000 calories a day instead of 2,500, human survival instincts will cause the body to adjust its energy needs according to the amount of available calories. Since the available ration is no greater than 2,000, and the individual can consume no more than that amount, the body will stabilise its energy expenditure by lowering its daily requirements. Weight loss will quickly be interrupted.

But the body does not stop there. Its survival instincts will drive it to take even greater precautions and start laying down reserves for possible future use. In other words, if the body is only given 2,000 calories, it will simply reduce its daily needs to, say, 1,700 and put aside 300 calories every day in the form of body fat. So, we obtain the opposite result from the one we had hoped for.

Paradoxically, even though the individual eats less, the body continues to store fat and progressively puts weight back on again.

The human body, constantly driven by its instinct to survive, behaves no differently from the hungry dog that buries its bone. A dog that is not being fed regularly, usually acts on its primitive instincts and hides food to create reserves in case things get worse.

How many of you have fallen victim to this unfounded theory of balancing energy input and output?

Among your acquaintances, you have certainly come across obese people who are actually starving themselves to death. The consulting rooms of psychiatrists are full of women being treated for depression resulting from the rigorous application of the calorie theory. From the moment that they begin to apply the theory, they enter an infernal circle from which they can never escape without putting back on even more weight than they have lost.

Some slimming professionals even run group therapy sessions, at which members are applauded for a couple of pounds lost and put to shame for a couple of pounds gained. The psychological cruelty of these practices harks back to the Middle Ages.

For the most part, doctors turn their backs on the problem. They realise that their patients are not losing weight, so they put it down to cheating and secret binges. It never seems to occur to them that the theory may be suspect.

In fact, physicians in general, are not particularly interested in the subject. I have noticed that, among the twenty or so doctors with whom I worked before writing this book, all had taken a specific interest in nutrition, and conducted research and experiments only because of their own serious weight problem.

What I find most disheartening, almost scandalous, is the way the general public has been allowed to go on believing that the calorie theory is scientifically proven. As a result, we have a situation where this theory has now become so accepted, it is one of the essential cultural elements of Western Civilisation.

The calorie theory is now so anchored in our minds that many cafeterias or local restaurants, to reassure clients, list the number of calories in each dish. Every week, at least one women's magazine features a new weight-loss method based on the calorie theory and designed by a group of professional nutritionists. These diets usually allow you a tangerine at breakfast, half a cracker at 11 o'clock, a chick pea for lunch and an olive for dinner.

It is amazing how the low-calorie approach has managed to con people for so long. I think there are two reasons for this.

First of all, a low-calorie diet always produces results. Food deprivation, the basis of the approach, inevitably leads to weight loss. However, as we have seen, the results are transient. Not only is a return to square one inevitable, but in most cases more weight is gained than is lost. The second reason is that "low-calorie" products today constitute an important market sector.

The exploitation of the theory, under the guidance of "qualified nutritionists," has turned into a tremendous market – one that primarily benefits the food industry and a few chefs who have lost sight of the true definition of gastronomy.

The calorie theory is false, and now you know why. But that is not the end of the story. The theory is so ingrained in your mind that you will inevitably catch yourself following its basic principles for some time to come.

When we begin to examine the new method of eating I am recommending in this book, you may well feel confused at first, because what I am proposing will seem to be in complete contradiction to this famous theory.

If this is the case, just reread this chapter until everything is quite clear to you.[2]

---

[2] See also the Technical Appendix p.199.

4

Where do those Extra Pounds Come From?

As we saw in the last chapter, the difference between "calories taken in" and "calories burned" does not explain our excess weight. In other words, the calorie theory does not explain how body fat is stored. There is another explanation, and that is the subject of this chapter.

INSULIN

Whether or not we accumulate body fat is directly linked to the secretion of insulin. *Insulin* is a hormone secreted by the pancreas, which plays a vital role in human metabolism. It acts on *glucose* (i.e. sugar) in the blood stream in such a way that the glucose is absorbed into the tissues of the body. The glucose can then be used either to satisfy the body's immediate energy needs or be stored as body fat.

So let us look at a few examples to see under what conditions and with what types of food body fat is likely to be produced, and to what extent.

INGESTING A CARBOHYDRATE

Let us take the example of a piece of white bread eaten on its own. White bread is a carbohydrate whose starch is broken down into glucose, which then passes directly into the blood stream. The body is suddenly in a state of hyperglycaemia[1] where glucose in the blood is raised above its normal level. The pancreas then automatically secretes insulin in order to:

1. Lower the amount of sugar in the blood stream (see chapter on hypoglycaemia) to its normal level of 1 gram per litre of blood.
2. Allow the glucose to be taken up by the body's tissues, either for short term storage as glycogen or as fat for long term storage.

[1] See Pt.3–Ch.1 on Hypoglycaemia; see also Technical Appendix 1 (Glycaemia) p.168

INGESTING A CARBOHYDRATE AND A LIPID

When for example, you eat a piece of bread with butter, the metabolic procedure is similar to the one described above.

The carbohydrate is broken down into glucose; the sugar level in the blood rises, so the pancreas secretes insulin.

However, there is a fundamental difference. In this case, the blood also contains fatty acids from the butter. If the pancreas is in perfect condition, the dose of insulin secreted will be exactly proportional to the amount of glucose to be treated. If, on the other hand, the pancreas is not functioning properly, the quantity of insulin released will be greater than the amount necessary to treat the glucose and subsequently a part of the lipid's energy (which under normal conditions would have been burned up by the body) will also be stored away in the form of fat reserves.

Insulin will thus trap not only the carbohydrate's energy, but that of the lipid as well. We can now understand that the difference between the person who tends to gain weight and the person who can eat anything without gaining an ounce, lies in the state of the pancreas. The former has a tendency toward hyperinsulinism.[2]

Storing as fat part of the lipids in the bloodstream, is not only dependent on the condition of the pancreas but also on the glycaemic index of the carbohydrate ingested.

Let us imagine that we are eating our piece of bread and butter on an empty stomach and that two situations are possible:

1. **The bread is white**. Since white bread has a high glycaemic index of 70, the sugar level in the blood will rise appreciably. If the pancreas is in poor condition, it will secrete too much insulin, trapping part of the fatty acids metabolised from the butter and storing them as fat reserves.

2. **The bread is made from wholemeal flour**. In this case, since the glycaemic index of wholemeal bread is low (35), the glycaemic curve will be modest. As a result, the insulin response will be weak. No abnormal storage of fat should therefore take place.

[2] See Technical Appendix p.208.

INGESTING A LIPID ON ITS OWN

Let us take as our example, a piece of cheese, eaten on its own.

The metabolising of a lipid on its own has no glycogenetic effect. In other words, no glucose is released into the blood stream, so the pancreas secretes hardly any insulin.

In the absence of insulin, there is practically no risk that the energy will be stored away as fat reserves.

This is not to say that ingesting a lipid on its own is of no consequence. During the digestive process, the body extracts all the essential substances from the lipid necessary for its energy producing metabolism, particularly the vitamins, the fatty acids and the minerals (such as calcium).

This example has been simplified on purpose. Even though prominent scientists helped me establish the principle, many may smile at its simplicity. I am sure you have already guessed that actually the process is slightly more complex.

But this simplification does emphasize the essential aspects of the nutritional phenomenon that are of interest to us. It explains the fundamental rules that will guide us through the weight-loss method. Although I consider this chapter to be of the utmost importance, because it shows how stored fats are created, we need more information to grasp fully how it is possible to continue eating "normally" yet "differently", so that you may lose those extra pounds and then maintain your weight at the desired level.

Note

In reality, the abuse of carbohydrates with a high glycaemic index frequently leads to hyperglycaemia causing pancreatic dysfunction. The hyperinsulinism that arises as a result, leads to an abnormal retention of fatty acids in the fat reserves.

It can be seen therefore, that a highly hyperglycaemic diet associated with the consumption of fats, will result in a progressive weight gain because of the hyperinsulinism which occurs.

5

Managing Your Stock

In the last chapter, we saw how we accumulate stocks of body fat. Now we will look at "why we put on weight."

You have seen that if the pancreas is not functioning properly, eating carbohydrate and lipid foods together can lead to excess weight. In fact, instead of talking about carbohydrates as a whole, I should have talked about "bad carbohydrates" specifically. For, as we saw in Part 1 – Chapter 2, it is the *type* of carbohydrate – *not the presence of carbohydrate as a broad category* – which lies at the root of the problem.

Maybe you know this already, but have probably never understood the scientific explanation for the phenomenon.

What you may not have realised either, is how you can apply these basic nutritional principles in order to reach and maintain your ideal weight.

Let us imagine that you are a man weighing thirteen and a half stone (about 86 kilos), and, taking into account your height[1], your ideal weight should be about eleven and a half stone (about 73 kilos). In other words, you are two stone (almost 13 kilos) overweight.

Well, it is true that some people are more corpulent and heavier than is "normal". However, this is the exception rather than the rule. Furthermore, even if they are made that way, it certainly does not mean that this new way of eating will not work for them. In fact, quite the reverse.

As with a good number of your contemporaries, when you were twenty to twenty-five years old, your weight was more or less ideal. After that, little by little, without you really realising it, you have gradually put on weight.

[1] See the calculation of the ideal weight p.198

The reasons are apparently the same for everyone: a change in lifestyle and a change in eating habits.

The first obvious change usually comes with marriage and a developing social life. However, it is more likely to be the new eating habits you cultivate in your professional life that will lead to the spare tyre around your waist, for your eating habits at work usually become very irregular. Later on, we will see why these habits are unhealthy.

Meanwhile, you weigh more than you should and you need to find a way to slim down.

First, since a rational mind always seeks to understand how things happen, we will start by looking at the purely technical aspects of the method.

The basic idea behind our method, is that we should not eat "bad" carbohydrates with lipids and we should take care to choose "good" lipids so as to avoid cardiovascular diseases. Further, as we shall see later on, the lipids should be consumed with a variety of vegetables containing a high proportion of fibre.

Here then, are some examples of balanced meals which contain no "bad" carbohydrates:

1. *Sardines* (protein + "good" fats)
   Mushroom omelette (protein-fats + fibre)
   Tossed green salad (fibre)
   Cheese (protein-fats)

2. *Smoked salmon* (protein + "good" fats)
   Lamb chop with string beans (protein-fats + fibre)
   Tossed green salad (fibre)
   Strawberries (fibre)

3. *Tomato salad* (fibre)
   Tuna with eggplant (protein + "good" fats + fibre)
   Tossed green salad (fibre)
   Cheese (protein-fats)

None of these meals contain any bad carbohydrates. Of course, the meals should *not* be served *with white bread*. And if you choose cottage cheese, *no sugar* should be added, unless it is an artificial sweetener[2].

But let us stay at the technical level for a moment, in order to discover how the weight is lost.

As was explained in the previous chapter, if the food does not contain any carbohydrates, the pancreas will not secrete insulin and as a result no fat reserves will be laid down.

Since the human organism needs energy to maintain its vital functions, to keep its temperature at 98.6° Fahrenheit and to move, it will draw on the stored fat reserves to release the amount of energy it needs.

So, as you continue to eat in a healthy way, consuming the vitamins, minerals and so on, the body will reduce the fat reserves which constitute your excess weight. It will meet its needs by first burning up the previously accumulated stocks of energy – namely body fat.

If you are a business manager, you already know the rules for administering stock: "last in - last out," "first in - first out". When "bad" carbohydrates are present however, the basic "stock rule" is never applied. Energy from "bad" carbohydrates, as we saw in the preceding chapter, is stored only for immediate use (last in-first out). Any surplus energy is stored away in the form of fat, and will remain there for a significant period of time.

If we exclude "bad" carbohydrates from our diets, then our bodies will automatically look to its fat stocks as a source of energy.

You are probably asking yourself what happens when the body has exhausted its fat stock.

Well, when you are "out of stock," so to speak, your body creates "a minimum buffer stock" that it will replenish as the need arises.

The human body, like the most sophisticated computer, will establish an optimal management program for its stored fats. But beware – the program is sensitive and easily upset by "bad" carbohydrates.

Nevertheless, you must not jump to conclusions and immediately

---

[2] Beware the composition of certain white cheeses, which often contain sugar. In addition, try to select white cheeses that have been well drained, since the whey contains lactose which is a carbohydrate.

assume that once you adopt these new eating habits, you will never taste pastries or other sweet foods again.

Bad carbohydrates can eventually be integrated into your diet, as long as you consume them in moderation and are aware of the dietary imbalances they create.

In the next chapter, we will learn how simple it is to indulge sensibly. We will see that once your system has completely reabsorbed your fat surplus and entered the stabilisation phase, you will be able to reintegrate bad carbohydrates into your meals containing lipids. However, you will have to be both careful and selective.

Your problem is that you are suffering from what is described medically as "*poor glucose tolerance*" This is the factor that distinguishes you who eat normally but "*run to fat*" and the next person who tucks in at every opportunity and stays as thin as a rake.

It is likely that for hereditary reasons[3] you are intolerant to sugars, but you are surely also one of the many victims of the deplorable eating habits of the society we live in. In all the industrialised countries, the preference for bad carbohydrates has become very marked over the past forty years.

You are probably addicted to (I will even go so far as to say intoxicated by) bad carbohydrates, and it will take some time for you to resume normal eating habits.

It all started during your childhood. Soft drinks, biscuits, sweets and lollipops. At snack time you ate enriched white bread with butter and jam, a chocolate bar, spongecake, or grandma's home-made fruit-cake. At college it was potatoes, pasta, rice and pizza, eaten on a regular basis. You needed nourishing foods that were filling and cheap. It was so much easier than preparing something like a vegetable soup. And anyway, everybody said sugar was good for your muscles.

For four years you lived on infamous student "fodder". You went to the fast food place across the road from the campus or had one of those improvised "get-togethers" at your "pad," which in reality was nothing more than a giant "carbo-feast".

---

[3] In a study of 540 adults adopted during childhood, showed that obesity is primarily a factor of heredity – New England Medical Journal, 1986.

And now you are fully engaged in a professional career, although the quality of your meals may have improved, you have remained a victim of bad eating habits.

At home you eat like the children, consuming those eternal chips, rice and macaroni cheese. It is rapid and it is so easy to prepare, particularly in this age of microwave technology.

At work things are no better. Like a true professional, when the morning meeting drags-on longer than anticipated, you ask your secretary to get some sandwiches to keep those hunger-pangs at bay.

And then, since you are always desperately trying to save time, you schedule meetings during your lunch hour and are forced to skip lunch altogether. You tell yourself that you will get something from the vending machines later. To keep going late at night or pick yourself up early in the morning, you must have your coffee – preferably strong and with plenty of sugar ... refined sugar of course, but then it is always good for the muscles, even when they are doing no work.

Then there are those famous business meals. With the help of your wonderful restaurant guides, you pick one of those "nouvelle cuisine" places that specialises in light cooking. But as soon as you get there, you are so hungry you cannot resist wolfing down the mini rolls with a generous pat of butter.

And then you have another cocktail party to attend. Another bind, though your host does serve some superb sausage rolls.

Weekends bring barbecues and pub meals with friends, and traditional family lunches. Grandma down in the country, does such wonderful roast potatoes, it would be a crime not to eat them all up with that delicious leg of lamb. And then there are the baked potatoes or the sirloin steak that tastes so much better with a generous helping of chips

So that is the story of how, just like the Michelin man, you manufactured your own tyre, a spare tyre which is as much an encumbrance at it is an eyesore.

And above all, it is the story of how you have become addicted to the wrong kind of carbohydrates, the ones that release far too much glucose into your blood stream.

So the time has finally come to rid your body of all these poisons and, coincidentally, to lose your excess fat.

It is a question of somehow raising your glucose tolerance threshold. At the moment this is very low, which means that the moment you consume the smallest amount of carbohydrate, especially "bad" carbohydrate, your pancreas gets to work manufacturing a disproportionate dose of insulin.

In other words, the amount of insulin produced by your body is no longer in proportion to the amount of glucose released into the blood stream. The excess insulin goes to work on some of the fatty acids and stores them as body fat. You are quite simply suffering the symptoms of hyperinsulinism[4].

But these famous bad eating habits that you have acquired, do not simply cause you to gain weight. They are also responsible for a large number of ailments you have suffered or are still suffering from, the most common being fatigue and poor digestion – both of which will be examined in greater detail in the chapters on hypoglycaemia and digestion.

At this point, I hasten to reassure you that this weight-loss method will not leave you weak, tired and light-headed as many other diets do. In fact, the exact opposite is the case. Providing you apply the simple guidelines properly, not only will you be losing weight, but you will also feel physically and mentally stronger, more dynamic and more able to cope with the stresses of your busy life.

The method is simple and practical. Even at the beginning, when you will have to eliminate certain foods from your diet, you will find that it is an easy method to apply in a restaurant, even when your mind is fully occupied with business matters. You may find it more difficult to apply the principles of the method at home, since it is not easy to change the eating habits of an entire household overnight. But when your spouse sees the results – maybe even reads this book – and understands how these eating rules can be applied, your whole family may come round to your views and adopt them enthusiastically.

As a general rule, theories are relatively easy to accept. The applications of those theories is usually more difficult. To help you do that, I will

[4] See Technical Appendix p.208

shortly examine the method in much more detail. However, just before we do that, perhaps you will bear with me a little longer, while we examine together the very serious topic of cardiovascular disease and its prevention.

6

Cardiovascular Disease Prevention

Cardiovascular disease is the number one cause of deaths in industrialised countries.

In 1982, 55% of all deaths in the United States were due to ischaemic cardiopathy and 16% were due to cerebro-vascular disease.

The impressive awareness campaigns put into place since 1963 have helped to lower cardiovascular diseases by 40%. However, the lowered mortality rate from cardiovascular diseases has not reflected a general decrease in the national mortality rate itself.

We can, however, notice that the diminution of the mortality rate from cardiovascular diseases is inversely proportional to the level of education, family revenue, and profession. What has been seen, in the end, is that the lower the income level, the higher the vulnerability to coronary heart disease. With the highest birth rate being among lower income families, we can only expect to see a steady increase of cardio-vascular diseases in the 21st century.

It is important to realize that the gravity of cardiovascular diseases varies from country to country in relation to the diet. It must be stressed that cardiovascular diseases have multiple causes and are not only linked to the cholesterol level, as people so often want to believe.

The different cardiovascular risk factors are as follows:

1) *high blood cholesterol levels*
2) *hypertriglyceridemia*
3) *hyperinsulinism and insulin resistance* (fat diabetes)
4) *free radicals*
5) *alcohol*
6) *smoking*
7) *salt*
8) *stress*
9) *coffee*

EXCESS CHOLESTEROL IN THE BLOOD

The cholesterol level has become a real obsession, almost to the point of paranoia, in some Western countries, notably in the United States. Contrary to popular belief, cholesterol is not an intruder in our body. In fact, more than 100 grams can be found in the human organism. Cholesterol is an indispensable fat, and it is only dangerous when present in excessive quantities.

Cholesterol is essential to cell functions. It ensures the fluidity and permeability of the cellular membrane. Cholesterol is a substance capable of converting itself in the liver into bile salts (important for digestion), in the adrenal glands into hormones (necessary to counteract stress) and in the skin into vitamin D (needed for healthy bone development).

Excess cholesterol in the blood is dangerous because it encourages the tendency for fat deposits to form (atheromas), weakens the arterial walls and narrows the diameter of blood vessels.

When this happens, the blood flow is slowed down. This creates vascular resistance which may give rise to different cardiovascular problems: angina, cerebrovascular disease, hardening of the arteries, high blood pressure, and in extreme cases, myocardial infarction (when the collapse of the vascular system suddenly obstructs the blood circulation).

It is important to know that human blood cholesterol has two origins: 70% is synthesized by the liver – that is to say, it is made by the body itself – and the other 30% comes from foodstuffs.

In other words, someone can have a diet consisting of only carrots and water and still find himself with a critical cholesterol level for other reasons. Professor Apfelbaum, one of the best known nutritionists, says that "alimentary cholesterol and blood-cholesterol are rarely related, and, for certain individuals, there is no relationship whatsoever..."

The absorption of alimentary cholesterol varies between 30% and 80%. The lower the cholesterol intake, the higher the hepatic synthesis. What this translates into is the formation of gall stones, with the risk of hepatic colics.

Good and Bad Cholesterol

Cholesterol is distributed in the blood by lipoproteins, which act as transporters. It is here that one must make a distinction between low and high-density lipoproteins

Low-density lipoproteins diffuse cholesterol to the cells and to the arterial walls, which are often the victims of fat deposits. LDL-Cholesterol is, for this reason, called "bad cholesterol."

High-density lipoproteins on the other hand, transport the "good" cholesterol (or HDL-Cholesterol), are responsible for cleaning the fat deposits out of the arteries.

The blood cholesterol norms are as follows:

- the LDL-cholesterol should be lower than 1.30g/l
- the HDL-cholesterol should be higher than 0.45g/l.
- the cholesterol total should be lower than or equal to 2g/l.
- the ratio of the total cholesterol level to HDL-cholesterol should be less than 4 : 1.

We know that the risk of cardiovascular diseases are twice as high if the cholesterol level exeeds 1.8 to 2.2 g/l, and four times as high if the cholesterol level is higher than 2.6 g/l. However, the total cholesterol level, as we have already seen, is not sufficient to make a noticeable difference in potential cardiovasculair risk; 15% of myocardial infractions are present in victims having a total cholesterol level between 1.5 and 2 g/l.

Fifty-three percent of American youngsters (in comparison to 21% of French children) aged between two and twenty have a total cholesterol level higher than 2 g/l, where the normal cholesterol level would be 1.60 g/l.

The autopsies performed on American GI's killed in Vietnam revealed that 40% of them had serious arterial lesions.

Women of childbearing years are protected from cardiovascular risks by hormonal secretions. However, vascular risks are multiplied nine times if the woman is taking an oral contraceptive. It is even more significantly increased if the woman smokes.

On the other hand, studies have shown that the mortality rate for men and for women is a lot higher when the cholesterol level is too low. In this case, the risk of cancer is multiplied by a factor of three.

Alimentary Cholesterol

Some foods contain varying quantities of cholesterol (see chart below for examples).

PER 100 GRAMS OF FOOD	CHOLESTEROL IN GRAMS
100 g of egg yolk	8.50 g
2 eggs of 50 g	9.63 g
beef kidney	0.43 g
caviar	0.34 g
shrimp	0.28 g
butter	0.23 g

It has been popularly believed, for a long time, that the daily cholesterol intake should not exceed 300 mg (as recommended by the World Health Organization). In fact, it has been shown since, that an additional daily cholesterol intake of 1000 mg only produces approximately five per cent increase in the blood cholesterol level.

It has been shown, in particular, that the consumption of 27 eggs per week has no effect upon blood cholesterol. This could be due to the high lecithin content of the eggs.

Only the reduced comsumption of saturated fats contained in foods can have an effect on the cholesterol level.

We have seen in Chapter 2 (Part One) that fats should be classified in three categories:

Saturated fats that are found in meats, poultry skin, milk, butter, dairy products and cheese
These fats indirectly increase the total cholesterol level, but especially the LDL-cholesterol. An interesting point to note, is that only the skin of poultry contains a significant percentage of saturated fats – not the flesh. So it is quite healthy to eat poultry without its skin, in preference to red meats.
While it is true that cheeses are high in saturated fats, their effects

are not as harmful as those of butter and whole milk. Professor J.M. Bourre stresses the fact that saturated fatty acids may combine with calcium to produce insoluble salts, thereby interfering in their intestinal absorption.

Mono-unsaturated fatty acids lower cholesterol. The best example is certainly oleic acid, found particularly in olive oil. It can be said that olive oil wins hands down in all categories when it comes to its beneficial action on cholesterol. Oleic acid is the only acid that succeeds in reducing the bad cholesterol (LDL) while at the same time increasing the good cholesterol (HDL).

Poly-unsaturated fatty acids from animal sources.are primarily found in fish oils. It was long thought that the Eskimos, who consume a lot of fish, were protected from cardiovascular disease by genetic factors. We then realised that it was the nature of their diet which gave them this protection.

The consumption of fish fats helps to lower the LDL-cholesterol level and triglyceride level. What is most important is that it aids the blood's fluidity, thereby reducing the risk of thrombosis. Their consumption in the form of gelatin capsules however, is much less effective.

Poly-unsaturated vegetable fatty acids are in corn oil, sunflower oil and wheat germ. They lower the total cholesterol level, particularly the LDL-cholesterol level and to a lesser degree, the HDL-cholesterol level. Some polyunsaturated vegetable fatty acids carry the essential fatty acids (linoleic acid, alpha-linolenic acid) and vitamin E.

HYPERTRIGLYCERIDAEMIA

When the level of triglycerides in the blood goes above 1.50 g/l, this can also be a factor in cardiovascular lesions. This excess of triglycerides can be linked directly to alcohol abuse or the excessive consumption of bad carbohydrates (sugar, white bread, corn, potatoes, soft drinks), as is generally the case in industrialised countries.

HYPERINSULINISM AND INSULIN RESISTANCE

As we have seen in the preceding chapters, the nutrients causing hyperglycaemia (too much sugar, too much white flour, too many potatoes, etc.) have put excessive demands upon the pancreas. This first shows up as hyperinsulinism (low tolerance to glucose), which can later evolve into fat diabetes, usually in association with obesity.

Now we know that insulin resistance is highly pathogenic for the arteries. The increase in blood platelet aggregation makes the blood flow less freely, making it more susceptible to blood clots that can block the arteries. In addition, the arterial walls become less flexible and the chances of LDL-cholesterol forming atheromas increase.

So you see that for there to be an effective treatment for a high blood cholesterol level, one must also adopt correct eating habits. To think otherwise is to delude oneself.

We can see then, that bad dietary habits – and particularly those inherent in the American-style of eating, – not only lie at the root of obesity but are also the cause of cardiovascular disease. To lay the blame for cardio-vascular disease wholly on fats, is mistaken as well as dangerous.

FREE RADICALS

Free radicals are substances that stimulate cell degeneration. Cell degeneration is often the cause of cancers and may also produce vascular lesions. Free radicals can be traced to a deficiency in selenium (whole cereals, fish, etc.), in vitamin L (sunflower oil, wheat germ oil, walnuts, hazelnuts, fish oils, etc.), in beta carotene (fruit and vegetables) and in vitamin C (fresh fruit and vegetables). Free radical increase the effect of LDL-cholesterol and its accumulation in the arteries.

ALCOHOL

An excess of alcohol has a harmful effect on the cardio-vascular system and induces arterial hypertension. However, it has been shown that a low alcohol consumption (one to three glasses of wine per day), has a beneficial effect on lipid metabolism, notably by raising the level of good cholesterol (HDL-cholesterol).

Professor Masquelier has shown that wines rich in tanin and containing pro-cyanide (such as red wines), lower the cholesterol level. Numerous studies have stressed that the populations of countries that drink wine regularly, such as France, Spain, Italy, and Greece, have a lower incidence of cardiovascular diseases than elsewhere.

TOBACCO

Tobacco is the cause of 25% of cardiovascular disease and is responsible for reducing the good cholesterol level (HDL-cholesterol). Thus, continuing to smoke when one already suffers from cardiovascular illness is truly suicidal.

SALT

Daily Needs

Our bodies need 3 to 4 g of salt per day. However, on average, we consume 10 to 13 g daily.

Salt and Obesity

Obesity results from an overload of fat, while salt interferes only in water metabolism.

There is, therefore, no evidence to suggest that obese people should follow a salt-free diet, especially in the case of women who complain about swollen hands or feet.

However, it is not advisable to have a diet with too much salt, as an excess of salt increases carbohydrate absorption in the intestine.

Salt and Cardiovascular Disease

Too much salt has been blamed for arterial hypertension. We now know this is true for only a proportion of the population; in fact, only 40 % of people suffering from high blood pressure get better by following a strict salt-free diet of less than 4 g per day.

As individuals react differently, the effects of a low-salt diet will vary.

On the other hand, very low-salt diets (less than 4 g per day) can be dangerous because they tend to lead to an increase in the total cholesterol (+11%) and LDLcholesterol (+ 1%) levels, which may increase cardiovascular risks.

STRESS

The stress of modern life results in the reduction of good cholesterol (HDL). It is important, therefore, to use effective stress management and relaxation methods.

COFFEE

Although the exact reason is still controversial, studies have shown that the ingestion of coffee (above six cups per day), whether it be regular or decaffeinated, raises the cholesterol level from five to ten per cent.

UNEQUAL CARDIOVASCULAR RISKS IN DIFFERENT COUNTRIES

One might be tempted to believe that in all the industrialised Western countries where there is an high standard of living, there would be approximately the same percentage of cardiovascular disease. This, however, is not the case. There are wide variations between countries, undoubtedly stemming from differences in local dietary habits. In the table below, it can be seen that Japan has the lowest incidence of cardiovascular disease, immediately followed by France.

As shown in the table above, France has a good record, bettered only by Japan.

To an American, subjected to short-sighted views on cholesterol and the bad reputation of fats, this might appear contradictory. In fact, the good showing of France can be directly linked to its dietary habits.

If you analyse the diet of the Irish (a country which incidentally, has one of the highest incidences of cardiovascular disease) and then compare it to that of the French, it is clear that it is not the quantity of fat that makes the difference, but the nature of the fat and the inadequate intake of vitamin C and fibre.

The Irish eat few green vegetables but a lot of potatoes. They use butter in their cooking, and are beer drinkers (beer is rich in maltose which has a glycaemic index of 110). The French, on the other hand, consume more green vegetables and fresh fruit, use oil (especially olive oil) instead of butter in their cooking, and drink red wine.

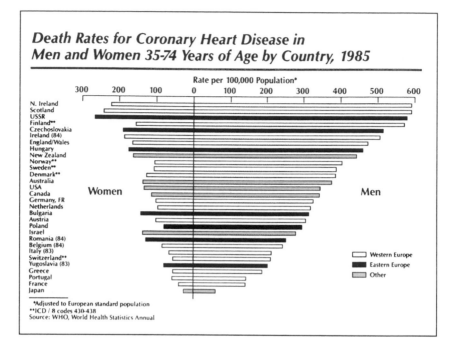

Death Rates for Coronary Heart Disease in Men and Women 35-74 Years of Age by Country, 1985

The countries that have the lowest incidence of cardiovascular disease are those that consume olive oil, fruit, pulses (lentils and beans) and drink wine. This is particularly the case for countries around the Mediterranean.

On the other hand, populations that have the highest incidences of cardiovascular disease, are those of Northern Europe (Denmark, Sweden, Norway, etc.) and English-speaking countries (United States, Canada, Britain, etc.). They are usually great consumers of hyperglycaemic foods (sugar, white flour, potatoes) and of beer. Their consumption of olive oil and of wine is very low, as is their consumption of green vegetables and fruit.

The various public awareness campaigns undertaken by a number of health authorities in the United States between 1962 and 1980, have brought about a significant improvement in the situation, with incidence of cardiovascular disease dropping by nearly 40%. While the Americans continue to focus on the relationship between fats and cardiovascular illness, they ignore the fact that the lack of the very fats they strive to eliminate from their diets could lead to grave deficiencies in essential fatty acids and vitamins A and E. Such an approach does not deal with the real problem.

The consequences of the American obsession with fats in the diet, together with the technical skill of a food industry which persists in removing all fats from food, may one day bring home the fact that moderation in these matters is the best philosophy.

If the French do not have high cholesterol levels and still eat foie-gras, cheese, olive oil, and drink wine, why indeed should these good foods be eliminated from the diet if this is what God, in his great wisdom, decided to give to us?

Conclusion

One should realize that, contrary to common belief, cardiovascular problems, especially those related to cholesterol, are not always what we thought they were in the past. To lay the blame solely on fats is not only wrong but dangerous. Such a short-sighted view can only serve to throw the patient's diet even more off-balance, without offering any effective solution. Having one believe, through the various anti-cholesterol campaigns and advertisements, that the problem can be solved by the simple exclusion of fats from the diet, is totally irresponsible.

There are certain important points to remember from this chapter:

1. Cholesterol is not the sole reason for cardiovascular illnesses. There are other factors such as hypertriglyceridaemia, insulin resistance, diabetes, free radicals, alcohol, tobacco, salt and stress.
2. Food-cholesterol represents only 30% of the total cholesterol level. Seventy per cent is synthesized independently by the liver from foods.
3. The cholesterol content in foods is not all assimilated by the body (as in eggs, for instance).
4. Saturated fats from nutrients are the real reason for a high cholesterol level. Thus, it is in this area that action must be taken.
5. On the other hand, there are certain fats that help lower the cholesterol level. Monounsaturated (olive oil) and polyunsaturated fats (fish fats or grain oils such as sunflower oil and wheat germ oil) are examples of these.

The best way to lower the cholesterol level is thus to change dietary habits:

- Reduce saturated fat consumption (meat, cooked meats, butter, whole dairy products).
- Eliminate the consumption of hyperglycaemic carbohydrates such as sugar, white flour, corn and derivatives of corn, and potatoes (whose glycaemic index is above 50).
- Consume monounsaturated (olive oil) and polyunsaturated fats (fish oils, grain oils).
- Increase consumption of whole cereals, especially wholemeal bread.
- Increase consumption of pulses (lentils, beans).
- Increase fish consumption (minimum of 300 g per week).
- Consume fibre regularly (fruit, vegetables).
- Strive for a sufficient intake of vitamins A, E, C, and selenium.
- Limit coffee consumption.
- Eliminate soft drinks and beer.
- Stop smoking.
- Decrease salt consumption.
- If possible, drink red wine (a maximum of half a litre per day).
- Control stress level by using an effective relaxation method.

PART TWO

The Weight-Loss Method

1

The Weight-Loss Method

We have finally reached the heart of the matter. The preceding chapters gave you a detailed overview of the technical explanations, but you are now probably impatient to know "how do I apply this weight-loss method?" So, without more ado, we will now see how to apply the guidelines that will help you achieve your goal: *to lose weight for ever without disrupting your social and professional life.*

But I must stress, especially to any of you who felt inclined to skip some of the preceding chapters, that they are absolutely essential if you are to apply the principles of the method logically and success fully. It is crucial that you understand the nutritional mechanisms described and rid yourself of popular notions on weight-loss, such as the calorie theory, which have inevitably influenced your thinking until now.

The weight-loss method has two phases:

1. *Actual weight loss*
2. *Maintaining that loss* or stabilising your new weight.

PHASE ONE
LOSING WEIGHT

Setting the goal

First and foremost, with a new undertaking – and an ambitious one at that – it is important to set yourself a clear goal.

First of all, you should establish how many pounds you are overweight (cf. page 198). Perhaps you already have a fairly clear idea of how much you would like to lose and probably many of you would be satisfied with a 10 pound loss, when really you need to lose 20 to 25 pounds.

For my part, I will encourage you to be more ambitious in the goals you set for yourself. You are determined and enterprising at work, so I urge you to be the same way with your own body. Would you be satisfied with a 4 or 5 per cent share of the market if your sales potential and marketing team were capable of reaching 12 per cent? Of course not! So adopt the same approach with your personal well-being.

You enjoy a challenge. Well then, take-up the gauntlet!

For some, a *quantitative* goal is perhaps not enough. Setting a *time* limit is also important. You want to lose so many pounds. Fine! However, how soon can that goal be achieved?

It is important to realise that every organism is different and the degree of response will vary from one individual to another, owing to a number of factors: sex, age, alimentary and nutritional history and heredity. It is therefore difficult to say how many pounds you will lose per week. Some may lose 2 to 4, others a little less. Moreover, in many cases the loss may be significant at first and then gradually slow down. So you should not worry if it takes you longer to lose weight than your colleagues.

Foods to be monitored closely

I know from experience that psychologically it is not good to begin anything on a negative note. So, for a long time I tried to explain to my friends the foods that were permitted before cautioning them against those that were not. However, this is a rather tedious approach, because the list of permitted foods is so long it never ends. The list of proscribed foods is much shorter and so much more important, it is better to start with that first.

Sugar

Sugar is the overall champion of bad carbohydrates. It should always be accompanied with a health warning, for it is a dangerous product when consumed in large amounts – which is precisely what happens these days, particularly with children.

In Part 3 of this book, I have dedicated a whole chapter to sugar, because it is essential you should be under no illusions about its nefarious role in matters of food. It is not only responsible for your excess weight, but it also leads to fatigue (see chapter on hypoglycaemia), diabetes, gastritis, ulcers, dental caries and coronary problems.

50

Perhaps you may think sugar is indispensable. Well, it is not. Just consider that for tens of thousands of years, sugar was not available to Man and he was no worse off as a result. In fact, the opposite was the case.

Less than 200 years ago, sugar was still a luxury product not available to the majority of the population. Today, sugar is everywhere, and it is just as dangerous as alcohol and drugs combined.

If you eliminate it completely from your diet you ask yourself, how you will you be able to maintain the minimum indispensable level of sugar in your blood stream.

Good question!

It is important to know therefore, that the human body does not need an external source of sugar (this is how the glycaemic level becomes upset). It can produce its own in the form of glucose when needed and is much happier operating that way. Glucose is, in fact, the body's only fuel.

As and when the body requires sugar, it produces the required amount from stored fats. The fats are simply transformed into glucose.

So, no more sugar!

You can either forget it completely, in which case you are to be congratulated, or you can replace it with an artificial sweetener.

Bread

I could have devoted an entire chapter to the subject of bread, because there is so much to say about it. "Good" bread that is, as opposed to the "poor" stuff that masquerades as bread on the majority of bakers' shelves these days.

Ordinary bread (not to mention all the packaged frozen dough) is made with bleached flour which is devoid of everything that a healthy metabolism requires in order to thrive. From the nutritional point of view, it contains very little – apart from energy in the form of glucose!

From the digestive point of view, it only brings trouble, since all the elements necessary for a healthy digestion have disappeared in the refining process.

The degree of whiteness of the bread indicates to what extent it has been refined, and the whiter the bread, the worse it is for your metabolism.

Wholemeal bread[1], or bread made the old-fashioned way with unbleached flour, is much more acceptable than white bread because it contains fibre. As a result, the quantity of glucose it releases is markedly lower than the amount released by white bread. It is therefore less "fattening".

However, despite the value of wholemeal bread, even this will be eliminated temporarily from cooked meals in Phase One. On the other hand, it should be eaten frequently at breakfast and with salad lunches. We will see why in more detail later on.

If you are worried about giving up bread, let me reassure you.

Should you eat white bread on a regular basis, as over 95% of people do, you have nothing to lose (but your excess pounds) when you give it up. In fact, you have everything to gain from such a wise decision, since refined flour is so bad for your health.

On the other hand, if you are used to eating only wholemeal bread or bread made from unbleached flour (which proves you already have some good eating habits), you may lose the benefits to be derived from fibre when you eliminate bread from your diet.

However, rest assured: not only will you continue to eat bread at breakfast and with salad lunches, but you will be encouraged to eat fibrous vegetables whose role as a substitute for whole wheat bread, is to ensure proper intestinal function.

Starchy Foods

Starchy foods are, for the most part, bad carbohydrates and must be excluded from your diet.

Potatoes

The number one starchy food is the potato. An interesting historical fact not widely know, is that when the potato was brought back from the New World, the French deliberately declined this tuber and gave it

---

[1] See Technical Appendix 1 p.170

to their pigs. They found it so awful they refused to eat it, even though the Germans, the Irish and the Scandinavians adopted it with enthusiasm. On the other hand, it must be said that these peoples didn't have much of a choice, as often there was little else to eat.

For two centuries, the French continued to scoff at what they called the "pig tuber".

It was not until 1789, during the French Revolution, when Parmentier, at the request of the revolutionary leaders, published his "Treatise on the Uses and Cultivation of the Potato", that the French finally decided to accept it. The famine at the time no doubt influenced their change of mind.

It was later discovered that, although the potato contains vitamins and mineral salts, it loses most of its nutritional qualities when cooked and particularly when peeled.

Recent experiments have shown that the potato releases a large amount of glucose when it is digested, because of the poor quality of its fibre.

Traditional nutritionists normally categorise the potato as a "slow sugar" which is incorrect. With respect to an index of 100 for pure glucose, it is possible to show that the potato has an index of 70[2]. So, despite the complexity of its carbohydrate molecule, the potato remains a bad carbohydrate (see Part One, Chapter 2). It has also been verified that processing the potato (as in instant mashed potatoes) raises the glycaemic index to 95.

So look upon the steaming potato on your neighbour's plate with the utmost contempt!

However, it is true, a chip is also a potato. Perhaps I am mistaken, but I have the impression you might be wavering already.

The fried potato is a carbohydrate-lipid, rather like buttered bread, and cannot be ingested without the risk of gaining weight, as the oil used for frying can be laid down as fat reserves.

So, think of steak and chips as a heresy!

Rid your mind of that diabolical combination! The lipid from the

---

[2] See Technical Appendix 1 p.171 and table p.10

meat and the bad carbohydrates in the chips constitute an unnatural combination.

I know it is not easy to give up this national dish, but it is the price you must pay to reach your goal. Believe me, when you do reach your ideal weight, you will not regret the sacrifice.

Once or twice a year – but not because I give way to temptation when I am confronted by a steaming plate of chips! – I deliberately decide to have some (when you no longer have a single ounce to lose, you can make decisions of this sort). However, since occasions of this sort happen only rarely, I like to savour them to the fullest and choose the best to be had.

If you do not know where to go, consult one of your restaurant guides, where I am sure the best chips in the country have already been selected for you. And if you want to keep damage to a minimum, order a salad to go with them. Not only is it delicious, but the fibre in the lettuce traps the starches, limiting the amount of glucose released and slowing down the rate at which the glucose is processed.

When you order meat in a restaurant get into the habit of asking what will be served with your dish. There will always something else other than potatoes. Ask for string beans, tomatoes, spinach, aubergine, celery, cauliflower, courgettes. ... And, if sadly there are only bad carbohydrates available, simply order a salad.

Dried Beans

Some may expect me to condemn dried beans unreservedly, given what was I have just said about the potato. Well, they are mistaken!

In the first version of this book in 1986, I ruled out dried beans, even when used to make a noble cassoulet[3].

I have since discovered with surprise and great satisfaction, the virtues of the bean. Henceforth, this food will be categorised as a good carbohydrate, given its very low glycaemic index[4].

In Phase One it can be eaten a breakfast or dinner, but of course without any fat like butter or lard. In Phase Two of course, it can be

---

[3] Cassoulet is a bean stew made with duck or goose preserves, comparable to pork and beans
[4] See Technical Appendix 1 p.171 and table p.10

eaten in reasonable amounts without restrictions and so once more I can enjoy my cassoulet.

White Rice

Rice, as it is traditionally eaten in Asia, is an unrefined grain that, by nature, contains all the essential elements needed for the maintenance of life.

But white rice, as it is eaten in the Western World, is highly processed. It is refined to the point that nothing remains of nutritive value except the one thing we could happily do without – starch.

Ordinary refined rice should be excluded from your diet, because, like refined flour, it is a bad carbohydrate that releases large amounts of glucose[5].

Brown rice, on the other hand, is allowed in Phase Two, but only so long as it is not ingested with lipids (i.e. cheese or butter). Brown rice, served with cooked tomatoes and onions, constitutes a healthy and balanced meal that everyone in the family will enjoy.

Unfortunately however, it is very difficult to find brown rice in restaurants.

Maybe it is because of its unaesthetic grey-brown colour or because it can take longer to prepare. Another problem with brown rice is that it takes a long time to chew, which can be quite inconvenient if you are trying to talk over a business meal!

Sweetcorn or Maize

Maize has been raised for centuries, yet humans have started to consume it on a regular basis only in the last few decades.

Forty years ago, not a single can of sweetcorn was to be found in Europe. It was cultivated exclusively for the purpose of feeding animals. In the United States, maize was used to fatten the livestock; until 1929 that is, when the drought that year decimated the herds and ruined the Midwest farmers. A true famine followed and, for lack of bovine meat,

---

[5] Glycaemic index of white rice = 70: brown rice = 50: sticky Asiatic rice = 20–40. See Technical Appendix 1 p.171.

the hungry people decided to eat the food originally intended for the farm animals – or at least what remained of it.

That is how America took to "corn", a habit exported to Europe in the aftermath of World War II.

We should not be surprised to learn that sweetcorn has a high glycaemic index of 70 (which makes it a bad carbohydrate), given the fact that for centuries it served to fatten cattle.

It is interesting to note that the industrial processing of maize considerably raises its glycaemic index, making popcorn and corn flakes particularly fattening, with and index of 85[6].

White Pasta

White Pasta is a bad carbohydrate. Even if white pasta is freshly made in the chef's kitchen, it should be excluded from every meal, because most of the time it is made from bleached flour. In addition, lipids are often added – butter, eggs, cheese and oils – making a "rich" pasta which results in a carbohydrate-lipid dish that only delays weight loss.

During the past few decades, Italian food has become more and more popular in Britain, where it is responsible, in part, for changing eating habits. Business meals are often organised in Italian restaurants.

I know it is unpleasant even to think about giving up pasta, especially when it is fresh and deliciously well-prepared. However, you should stay clear of it and resist the temptation to indulge.

If, unfortunately, you are served fresh white pasta (any other kind of white pasta is not even worth considering), try to refuse whilst you are still in Phase One, the weight-loss phase. When you are cruising along at your ideal weight in Phase Two, eat it only if you are sure it is worth the sacrifice.

Whole wheat pasta made from unrefined flour, may be eaten in Phase One, but lipids should be excluded from the sauce. This limitation can be relaxed in Phase Two and I will tell you later how the pasta should be prepared and when ideally it should be eaten.

Whole wheat pasta is, in fact, categorised as a good carbohydrate, since the glycaemic index is only 40.

[6] See Table p.10

It is regrettable though that in France this product should be wrongly sold as a health food item and therefore at two to three times the price of normal pasta – a scandalous swindle, since the cost of producing whole wheat pasta does not even include the expense of industrially bleaching and refining the flour.

In Germany, whole wheat pasta is sold at the same price as normal pasta, so let us hope that the opening of European frontiers will soon rectify the situation in France.

Other bad carbohydrates

I have purposely elaborated on the main carbohydrates which are eaten regularly and are bad for you, and which must be given up at least for the time being.

However, there are other carbohydrates to be avoided and you will find a full list of these at the end of Chapter 2, in the first part of this book. You should familiarise yourself with this list, so that if ever you run into them on a menu, in a dish or on your plate, you can avoid them. Random examples of these are semolina and refined breakfast cereals, often made with fats, sugar and other caramels, which we often eat at breakfast to salvage our conscience.

Lentils, chick peas and other split peas are different, in that they only release small amounts of glucose during digestion[7]. They may be eaten in Phase One without fat, but in Phase Two they can be reintegrated into your normal diet and eaten with meat dishes.

In addition, there is a rather particular carbohydrate that I would now like to examine: fruit.

Fruit

There are certain subjects you discuss at your peril and fruit is one such, for were I so ill advised as to suggest that it should be eliminated from your diet, a good number of you would be so scandalised, you would close the book at this point and read no further.

Fruit is a symbol in our culture; a symbol of life, health and prosperity.

[7] See Technical Appendix 1 p.171

Fruit is a source of many vitamins. At least, that is what we think.

Let me assure you straight away, we are not going to eliminate fruit. However, you will have to learn to eat it differently in order to enjoy the benefits without suffering the drawbacks, since fruit is much harder to digest than you might think.

Fruit is a fibre but also a carbohydrate, containing sugar in the form of fructose. And we must pay very careful attention to fructose because it transforms itself easily into glycogen (which is a form of energy immediately available to the body). Fortunately, the amount of sugar is not very great and in any case it is released into the metabolism in small amounts because of the fibre contained in the fruit. The amount of energy that therefore results is not very alarming, but it is energy that is ready for immediate use. The important rule to remember here (and if you remember only one rule in the book, retain this one) is that fruit should never be combined with lipids or proteins.

This observation is not made solely as a result of our concern to lose weight. It is derived from the laws associated with the chemistry of digestion, for when fruit is consumed with lipids or proteins, not only does it interfere with the digestion of those other foods but it also loses most of its own nutritional value (vitamins, etc.). This is why the biggest mistake one can make, is to eat fruit at the end of a meal.

As I suspect you may be somewhat sceptical at this point, I will explain myself more thoroughly.

When fruit is consumed with lipid-proteins such as meat or cheese, it will remain blocked in the stomach with them instead of passing rapidly into the intestine where it would normally be digested.

Meat remains in the stomach for 2 to 3 hours, where it undergoes the most important phase of its digestion in the presence of essential enzymes. The fruit remains imprisoned with it in the stomach, where in the presence of heat and humidity it ferments and eventually produces alcohol.

If this is allowed to happen, the whole digestive process will be upset. In the first place, the fruit will lose all its nutritional value: and then, since it never rains but it also pours, the lipid metabolism will also be upset leading probably to abdominal bloating.

Fruit must therefore always be eaten on its own!

This is one rule we all should have learned in school. Had we done so, we would have had fewer upset stomachs, though at that age our bodies would have been more able to compensate. But for an adult – and especially an older person – fruit at the end of a meal can be a real poison.

So when can we eat fruit?

On an empty stomach. In the morning, for example, before breakfast. However, you will have to wait 20 minutes before eating a carbohydrate breakfast with cereals.

In Phase One however, it is advisable not to have fruit before a protein-lipid breakfast.

You can also eat fruit late at night, at least two or three hours after dinner. For those who habitually suffer from insomnia (which ought to be less of a problem after following the eating method set out in this book), it is better to avoid oranges before you go to bed, since vitamin C is a stimulant and can keep you awake.

Fruit can also be consumed some time in the afternoon. Make sure that it is well after lunch (about three hours) and still a long time before dinner (at least one hour).

You can even eat a meal consisting only of fruit, as long as you eat nothing else.

I will conclude my discussion on fruit by emphasising one last detail. If possible, always eat the skin of the fruit. Most of the fibre, that benefits the intestinal tract, (and even some vitamins) are found in the skin.

Eating fruit with the skin lowers its glycaemic index, so you will lose more weight (or gain less) if you respect this last rule.

Finally, among the foods to be monitored closely we will study drinks. To begin with, let us look at alcohol.

Alcohol

Alcohol is fattening! This is what you believe because this is what you have been told. You have often been made to feel guilty by the insidious claim that your excess weight has been caused by alcohol. Let us therefore examine the question objectively.

It is true that alcohol is fattening, but much less fattening than sugar, white bread, potatoes or white rice. This is why, very soon after having lost your excess pounds, you can reintroduce wine into your diet in moderate amounts.

Alcohol is fattening because it is a carbohydrate that is rapidly stored in the form of fat immediately after it has stimulated the secretion of insulin. This is particularly the case when it is consumed on an empty stomach. However, when the stomach is already full, particularly with protein-lipids (meat and cheese), alcohol is metabolised at a slower rate and combines with other foods thus producing fewer fat reserves.

It is essential that you give up aperitifs. In Phase One, if you feel constrained to drink with your guests, choose a non-alcoholic drink like tomato juice or sparkling water with a slice of lemon.

The only noble aperitif to my mind, is a glass of good champagne. But I beg of you, never let them put a blackcurrant liqueur or any other bizarre syrup in it, either to hide its mediocre quality or emphasise the originality of the establishment.

So, if you cannot help yourself, accept a glass of good champagne, but above all *do not drink it on an empty stomach*. Nibble on the snacks first.

However, be careful. Choose snacks that are free of carbohydrates: olives, cheese, dried meats (dry salami, for instance)[8] but stay clear of crisps, peanuts and crackers.

It must be said however, that in Phase One you should try to exclude aperitifs completely. It is necessary to abide by the stringent rules of these first few weeks in order to maximise your weight loss.

After Dinner Drinks

Cross these drinks out. Cognac, Armagnac and many liqueurs may be delicious, but from every point of view they are also very bad for your metabolism.

Maybe you like to think that these after dinner drinks will help you to digest your meal. Well, let me assure you, when you have successfully

[8] Those with cholesterol problems should exclude dried meats and cheeses other than the low-fat variety. See Technical Appendix p.188.

adopted the dietary principles contained in this book, you will have no problems in digesting your food even after the most lavish meal.

Beer

As far as beer is concerned, I am unable to be any more lenient. It is a drink that should be taken in very modest amounts.

Just as you may know people who wolf down carbohydrates by the ton and never gain an ounce, you have certainly met heavy beer drinkers whose stomachs remain incredibly flat. The wife of one of my closest friends is just such a person!

However, it is not necessary to have visited Germany to be aware of the secondary effects of drinking too much beer: bloating, weight gain, bad breath and indigestion, despite the presence of diastases – small enzymes that are specifically designed to help the digestion process. Let's just say that without diastases, beer-drinking would be catastrophic.

We should be wary of what beer contains: alcohol (admittedly in small quantities), gas, and especially a substantial amount of maltose (4 g per litre), a carbohydrate with a glycaemic index of 110 – higher even than glucose! Furthermore, the combination of alcohol and sugar can easily lead to hypoglycaemia, which lies at the root of fatigue and under-achievement (see chapter on hypoglycaemia). Beer therefore has a high energy potential easily converted into fat reserves. If you are a heavy beer drinker, give up the habit, especially between meals. If however, you really cannot resist, approach the problem as you would do with chips. Indulge yourself once or twice a year, drinking a couple of pints of the very best beer on offer at your favourite pub. However, remember: never do it on an empty stomach!

In Phase One, eliminate beer completely. However, in Phase Two – as we will be reintroducing a moderate amount of wine into our regime – you may choose to drink a half-pint of beer with your meal instead.

Wine

I have saved wine till last, because it is the only alcoholic drink that I favour.

It is a noble drink which deserves to be held in high esteem. However, be wary of "vin de table" or table wine, and other nameless brews enriched with sulphur anhydride, likely to burn your stomach and conjure-up headaches.

Choose rather a wine that spells out its origins – particularly if they are synonymous with quality and you can afford it. Remember that wines rich in tannin contain a substance called procyanidine which lowers the level of cholesterol in the blood. Choose red wines therefore rather than white, for their more positive effects on cholesterol. I appreciate Sancerres, Chablis and white Burgundies as much as you, but they are sometimes a bit more toxic than reds. Moreover, be aware of the quality of the white wine you drink. A low quality white wine, depending on the sensitivity of the individual, will often provoke headaches or insomnia (especially in women)[9]. Red wine, particularly Bordeaux, can be introduced into your regular diet as long as you do not drink excessively (about half a litre a day).

However, in Phase One, be strict: only drink wine if you must and then very rarely.

In Phase Two, you can consume it on a daily basis and not worry about gaining weight. However, when you drink wine, take into account the amount of other carbohydrates you consume. I am thinking specifically of chocolate and other desserts that we will study in detail later on.

In Phase One, the restrictive phase, it may be difficult for you to attend a business meal without having a drop of wine. If you announce from the outset that you do not drink, you may offend or annoy your colleagues.

My advice is as follows: allow your glass be filled, handle it as if you were drinking, but only moisten your lips. Do not drink. If it is a fine wine, this will allow you to enjoy the bouquet longer! It will not prevent you from sharing a good wine with your friends and indulging in the pleasantries that go with it.

I have tried this method many times over a number of weeks, and believe me, nobody ever noticed I was not drinking.

In the same way, no one has ever noticed that I never eat bread. I

---

[9] Bad champagnes have the same effect. Drink only top quality brut. Severe headaches usually result from the fermentation process having been interrupted, when sulphur anhydride is released. This is particularly true of rosés.

always take a roll from the basket, break it in half, and leave it next to my plate.

Coffee

Really strong coffee, Italian espresso containing sufficient caffeine to awaken the dead, is absolutely forbidden. Drink decaffeinated or light American-style coffee. You can find "decaf" almost anywhere, and usually it is quite good. Even serious coffee drinkers can hardly tell the difference.

If you are an enthusiastic drinker of very strong coffee, it is undoubtedly because you regularly feel the need for a stimulant to wake you up.

If you regularly get tired at around 11 o'clock in the morning or in the middle of the afternoon, the chances are you are hypoglycaemic (see the chapter on hypoglycaemia).

Considerable care should be exercised when consuming food and drinks containing caffeine, because a significant number of people are very sensitive to it. Even though it is not a carbohydrate, it stimulates the secretion of insulin from the pancreas. If you have just finished a meal free of bad carbohydrates, and all surplus energy is on the verge of being discharged from the system, it would be foolish to drink a strong cup of coffee, cause the pancreas to secrete insulin, and trap the energy from the food you have just consumed.

If you are a habitual coffee drinker, you will have no trouble switching to decaffeinated coffee and soon enough, you will be surprised to find that you have forgotten about coffee completely.

As you know, serious coffee drinkers (caffeinated or decaffeinated) expose themselves to an additional risk: that of raising the cholesterol level in their blood.

Soft Drinks

Colas, fizzy and other soft drinks are usually made from synthetic fruit or plant extracts, and all contain a lot of sugar.

They should be excluded from your diet, not only because they contain sugar, but because they also contain artificial gas that causes stomach aches, gastritis, and aerophagia.

Even if the extracts are natural, the drink, unless it is sugar-free, is still toxic. Even in the natural extracts from citrus fruits, there are often important traces of noxious substances like terpene.

The worst soft drinks are sugared colas. Like cigarettes, they should carry a government health warning.

Doctor Emile-Gaston Peeters[10] has warned that:

"Every bottle (approximately 19 centilitres) of cola contains about 21 mg of caffeine and 102 mg of phosphoric acid. Caffeine is a strong stimulant and phosphoric acid is very acidic. The high phosphoric concentration risks upsetting the balance between calcium and phosphorus in the normal diet, which in turn can lead to a serious calcium deficiency in the bones. Finally, one must be certain that the phosphoric acid does not contain any important traces of toxic heavy metals. The conclusion is simple: *Children and adolescents should be encouraged not to drink cola.*"

As far as diet soft drinks are concerned, they are obviously less harmful because of the absence of sugar. But what was said about colas, sugar-free or not, still holds true.

Milk

Milk is a carbohydrate-lipid, containing both fats and carbohydrates. In Phase One it is better therefore to drink only skimmed milk.

The carbohydrates are found in the whey. In the cheese-making process, they are lost and only lipids and proteins remain.

Non-fat cheese contains only proteins and other substances that are of no interest to us here.

Fruit Juices

I will not deal with fruit juices at length because the previous discussion on fruit also holds true here. They are carbohydrates and should be treated as such.

I would, however, advise you to choose fruit in preference to fruit

---

[10] *Le Guide de la Diététique*, published by Marabout.

juice so as not to lose the benefits of the fibre in the pulp. In sum, only home-made fruit juices made from fresh fruits are acceptable. Never consume the commercial pseudo-fruit juices, which are overly acidic, completely devoid of natural vitamins and, for the most part, sweetened with sugar.

2

Phase One – Applying the Method

Phase One of this method is not necessarily difficult to apply, since it simply consists of eliminating certain foods from your diet. But in order to succeed completely, you need to have a thorough understanding of the *basic principles* presented to you in this book.

I know from experience that this is where many fail. I am not doubting your intelligence or your ability to assimilate new concepts, but in this particular case, it is important to rid oneself of those preconceived ideas which are so deeply ingrained in our subconscious that they have become part of our "cultural heritage." The simple ideas presented here, based on elementary scientific and medical principles, have not yet been generally appreciated, so you cannot count on those around you for help in your enterprise.

For instance, you need to remember that if you eat a proteic-lipidic meal (meat or fish with a helping of vegetables), you can eat cheese with a clear conscience[1] (providing you do not exaggerate, of course), and without breaking any of the new eating rules you have learned.

If, on the other hand, you want to eat cheese during a carbohydrate meal, you may only eat non-fat cheese.

What now follows, is a guide to help you apply the principles of Phase One.

BREAKFAST

Breakfast – Version One

A *carbohydrate* breakfast:

– *fruit* (at least 20 minutes before the rest of the meal),

[1] This is true only if your cholesterol level is normal (See Part One – Chap.6 and Technical Appendix)

— *wholemeal bread,*
— *non-fat cottage cheese,*
— *decaffeinated coffee or weak tea,*
— *skimmed milk,*
— *artificial sweetener* (if necessary).

The breakfast suggested here contains no lipids and is made up only of good carbohydrates with a low glycaemic index.

Let us take a closer look at what it does contain:

Fruit

You may choose any fruit. Personally, I would recommend an orange, two tangerines or even kiwis, because vitamin C is very efficient on an empty stomach.

If you choose an apple, eat it slowly with the skin.

A banana, too rich in carbohydrates, is not a good option.

Be sure to wait 20 minutes between the fruit and the rest of your breakfast. I would suggest you eat the fruit when you get up, before you wash and dress – which should take you at least half an hour – and then sit down for the rest of your meal.

Fruit in Phase One is optional, and your weight loss does not depend on it.

If you never eat fruit, which is a pity, do not go out of your way to do so because I mention it here. However, if you are used to eating fruit every day and do not want to give up the habit, then – as I remarked earlier – one of the rare moments you can eat fruit is in the morning on an empty stomach. You can, if it is convenient, eat only fruit for breakfast. On the other hand, if you pick *Breakfast – Version 2*, the proteic-lipidic breakfast, you should eat your fruit at least one hour beforehand.

Wholemeal bread

You should only buy wholemeal bread – preferably from totally unrefined flour, which in France is known as "farine integrale". Unfortunately, this grade of flour is not widely available and most wholemeal bread is made from partially refined flour, containing sometimes as little as 25% unrefined wheat.

To distinguish wholemeal bread with a high percentage of unrefined flour, called "pain complet" in France, look for a rough texture. Do not judge solely on the outer colour of the loaf, since refined flour can be coloured artificially. Alternatively, if you like it, you can also buy, what the Germans call "schwartzbrot". It is generally dark and has a rough and grainy texture.

Wholemeal bread absorbs gastric juices more rapidly, so you will very quickly feel satisfied. Since I never specify the quantity of food you should eat, I could be tempted to tell you to eat as much as you want. In fact, I will be content to advise you to eat "reasonably".

You can also eat grilled whole wheat rolls, similar to the Swedish variety, or even crackers. There are several brands on the market, but it is important to chose a product that contains no added sugars or fats. Similarly, if you buy rusks, make sure they are made from wholemeal flour and contain no sugars or fats.

If you like biscuits, they too should be made from wholemeal flour and contain neither sugars or fats – a fairly rare phenomenon!

Now we come to the problem of what you put on your bread.

In Phase One, you should not spread butter or margarine on your bread, as you will be allowed to do in Phase Two. Instead, use non-fat cottage cheese, with a dash of salt or sweetener if you cannot stand its blandness. Alternatively, you can spread Greek non-fat yoghurt on your bread before topping it with sugar-free jam. For those with a sharp tooth, the combination is addictive.

Normal jam and unfortunately honey, are bad carbohydrates because they contain a lot of sugar. So they too must be given up. In their place, you can use sugar-free jams, made either with fructose but preferably with juices extracted from fruit like apples or pears. These latter jams can be quite delicious, much better than those made just with sugar.

You may prefer to eat cereal in the morning. Again, I urge you to choose whole grain cereals that do not contain any undesirable additives such as sugar, honey, fats or oilseeds, etc. Read the ingredients printed on the package carefully. In any event, you should rule out all white rice and corn based products. Choose, instead those that are rich in fibre,

Decaffeinated coffee or weak tea

I cannot stress enough the importance of abstaining from drinking strong coffee. Weak coffee will do. It would be even better if you could get used to drinking decaffeinated coffee with ground chicory. If you drink tea, make sure it is not too strong, since tea also contains caffeine.

Skimmed milk

If you put cream in your coffee or tea, use only skimmed milk. Even partially skimmed milk should be avoided, because it contains lipids. Powdered skimmed milk is your best bet, because you can obtain a highly concentrated mix.

It goes without saying, you should put no sugar in your coffee or tea. If you really have to, use only an artificial sweetener.

BREAKFAST

Breakfast – Version Two

This breakfast is *proteic-lipids*. It contains *no carbohydrates* – either good or bad.

I suggest you use this one when you are staying in a hotel, as the carbohydrate *Breakfast – Version One* is not always easy to apply when you eat out[2]

Breakfast – Version Two includes the following choices:

– *eggs*
– *bacon, sausage and/or ham,*
– *cheese,*
– *decaffeinated coffee, weak coffee or weak tea,*
– *skimmed milk or cream*
– *artificial/sweetener (if necessary)*

This has much in common with the traditional British breakfast – but without the fried bread, cereal or jam, of course.

---

[2] If you suffer form high blood cholesterol, this breakfast choice is not recommended. Those who do not have a cholesterol problem should take care to balance their consumption of lipid (See Part One – Chap. 6 and Technical Appendix)

It is crucial that you exclude all carbohydrates in this breakfast.

As you already know, lipids contain a lot of potential energy. They will be completely burned and disposed of only in the absence of insulin. Remember therefore, *insulin is secreted in the presence of carbohydrates or a stimulant such as strong coffee or tea.* Be careful not to err.

LUNCH – (Phase One)

Lunch, eaten outside the home most of the time, will be almost invariably *proteic-lipidic* and rich in fibre. However, this is not to say that you should eat a lot of fats – in fact, quite the opposite (see "good" and "bad" lipids p.38).

To help you avoid making any mistakes, I will give you a few examples as to how you should go about things. However, when you decide what you will be having for lunch, I recommend strongly you consult Table 1 (p.153) for a brief list of permitted foods. You can even photocopy the list and carry it with you. Very soon you will have it memorised.

Here is a *typical lunch* menu:

- *raw vegetables,*
- *fish and/or meat,*
- *authorised vegetables* (see list),
- *salad,*
- *cheese,*
- *to drink: still water* (sparkling water should be avoided).

Starters

Any type of salad is acceptable, as long as none of the ingredients is a carbohydrate. Be sure that what your orderdoes not contain *potatoes, sweetcorn, rice, carrots that have been cooked or beetroot.* The ideal sort of salad is the one that originated in Southeast France but is now widely known in Europe, called "Salade Niçoise". This salad contains lettuce, tuna fish, tomatoes, olives, hard-boiled eggs, anchovies and olive oil, and not only is it the ideal for someone following my method, but it is also delicious.

In Phase One, you should avoid carbohydrate-lipids like nuts. So do not order a salad with walnuts. Bacon bits are allowed, but fried bread in the guise of *croutons* is most definitely not! Be very much on your guard in a restaurant – particularly in France – because many restaurateurs have a strange obsession with croutons!

Be vigilant. Do not tolerate any slight errors by the restaurant staff, they may well be major ones as far as your regime is concerned. After all, you do not allow mistakes at work to go by default and you are no push-over for your secretary or employees. So why be lenient with the restaurant waiter? If you asked for a salad "without croutons," or "without sweetcorn", that is what you should get!

If you want the maître d'hôtel or the waiter to take you seriously, make sure they understand that you will only accept what you specifically ordered. If you want to get your message across with the minimum of fuss, tell the maître you are allergic. It is an approach I have found works every time!

As long as your salad contains string beans, leeks, artichokes, cabbage, cauliflower, tomatoes, endives, asparagus, mushrooms, radishes, etc., eat to your heart's content. However, be sure to avoid beetroot since it contains a lot of sugar.

You can also eat as many eggs as you wish, even if they are served with mayonnaise[3].

Tuna, sardines in oil, crab, prawns, salmon (smoked or marinated) can all be ordered as an hors d'oeuvre. Never-the-less, you should avoid oysters, scallops and "foie gras"[4] while you are still in Phase One. They all contain some carbohydrates which could slow down the process of losing weight. In Phase Two however, there are no such restrictions.

The Main Course

The main course is essentially made up of meat or fish. On these foods there are no restrictions, except with regard to their preparation

You should never order breaded meat or fish. Bread crumbs are bad carbohydrates. Also, beware of fish that is rolled in flour before it is

---

[3] When you buy mayonnaise, read the label on the jar to make sure it contains no sugar, glucose or flour. In a restaurant, make sure the mayonnaise is made on the premises in the traditional way. Surprisingly, often this is the case.

[4] "Foie Gras" is a gourmet paté made with high quality goose and duck liver. When you have moved from Phase 1 to Phase 2, if you ever come across the freshly made version as opposed to the tinned, you should indulge yourself. It is a gastronomic treat not to be missed!

cooked. Always ask for grilled, poached or steamed fish. Avoid cooking fats that have become "saturated" through being heated. Though they make the dish unnecessarily greasy and are not always easy to digest, they should be avoided mainly for their bad effect on cholesterol levels in the blood.

Pay particular attention to sauces! If you are accustomed to "Nouvelle Cuisine", you will know that the sauces are generally light because they do not contain flour and are produced by deglazing the cooking pan with low fat "crème fraîche". This makes them particularly suited for use in Phases One and Two. By the same token, sauces made with flour should be excluded.

If you eat meat, you can order a bearnaise sauce if you wish, providing it has been made on the premises in the traditional way[5]. But do not have mustard in Phase One, as it is made from the flour of the mustard plant and is therefore a carbohydrate. Eaten in small quantities, it can be included in Phase Two without affecting your weight. However, in Phase One it is liable to destabilise a sensitive metabolism.

As a general rule, you should be suspicious of all industrial sauces available in popular restaurants, as they often contain large amounts of sugar. This is particularly true of ketchup and all spicy sauces served in seafood restaurants.

Select fibrous vegetables if they are an option. You can choose from a never-ending list including tomatoes, courgettes, string beans, aubergines and cauliflower. Become familiar with the list in Table 1 (p.153).

As I said before, if there is nothing else on the menu, order salad. Iceberg lettuce, curly lettuce, red-leaf lettuce and endives are all acceptable. You can eat as much as you want, as a starter, as an entree or as a side-dish.

But, beware of the dressing you choose. Thousand Island, Blue Cheese, French and other dressings common in Britain and other North-European countries usually contain a large amount of sugar. Even "vinaigrette" may have sugar added by the restaurant, particularly if the vinegar is sharp. The safest way is to make your own. This is quite easily done by

[5] Industrially produced béarnaise will normally contain sugar, flour and preservatives, in which case it should be excluded from your meal. So read the label carefully!

having the ingredients brought to the table. In a dessert spoon add salt and vinegar or lemon, mix with your fork until the salt is dissolved and spread evenly over the salad. Trickle oil over the leaves and work the vinaigrette lightly into the salad with your fork and spoon. Nothing could be simpler.

Cheese

In most restaurants, the menu offers a dessert or cheese option. In Phase One, limit yourself to the cheese. And you should eat the cheese without bread. This is not impossible, and you will soon see that it is much more enjoyable eaten this way. Soon enough you will be able to enjoy your cheese with a glass of red wine.

In countries like France and Italy, you will have noticed that cheese is accorded the honour of being eaten with a knife and fork – a practice that should be encouraged in Britain, in that has the added advantage of ensuring that the waiter is not over-miserly with the portions of cheese.

In Phase One, just about every cheese is allowed – unless you happen to suffer with high cholesterol, when of course, you should restrict yourself to low-fat cheeses. However, I have some reservations about Cantal[6] and goat cheese for now, since they contain small amounts of carbohydrate.

Drinks

In Phase One, as we have already seen, it is important to eliminate all alcoholic drinks, including wine. Drink water or herbal tea if you wish. But avoid sparkling waters, because the carbonic acid they contain will cause bloating and upset the digestive process.

In any case, I suggest you drink very little water during your meals or you may drown your gastric juices and upset the digestive process. If you are really thirsty, do not drink water until you are at least mid-way through your meal. On no account should you drink water before you start to eat. It is a bad habit we all have, and it is responsible for many of our digestive problems. Instead, we should make a point of ensuring an adequate intake of water between meals.

If you attend business meals while you are in Phase One, remember

---

[6] Cantal is a French cheese that is produced in the Massif Central, the central region of France.

that you must skip the alcoholic cocktails. Order tomato juice, and if you absolutely must accept something alchoholic (if for example, a cocktail has been prepared for everyone), be sure not to drink it. Pretend to do so by putting your lips to the glass, but never actually swallow. Eventually you will be able to put your cocktail down somewhere casually where no one will notice. If this is not possible, be creative. Place your glass in front of one of those heavy drinkers who will always confuse their glass with yours – especially if it is full. Should this type of person happen not to be around, which would surprise me, there is always the flower pot, the champagne bucket, the window (if it is summer time) or the basin in the cloakroom.

If you are at a cocktail party and you are still in Phase One, this then, is the plan of campaign:

You accept the glass of champagne you have been given, putting it to your lips but not drinking it, until eventually you manage to set it down somewhere and "lose" it.

Food served at cocktail parties can often be a problem as well.

You can eat the salmon, the salami, the egg or the asparagus on the bite-sized sandwiches, but you must be clever enough to separate the bread from the rest and then dispose of it somehow. Not always an easy task, but look on it as a challenge to your ingenuity! If all else fails, then accept defeat gracefully and tuck into the inevitable army of cheese cubes with cocktail sticks "at the present".

Alternatively, engage the sausages in mortal combat! I would be surprised if there were none of these available. Little cocktail sausages are always served at these affairs. Dig in and eat as much as you want, so long as you are sure they do not contain flour. However, watch out for the mustard!

If you think you cannot resist a bountiful table of food, if you think you will immediately give in because you are hungry, here is a solution. Before you go to the party, nibble on something that you are allowed to eat, just to fill your stomach.

This wise advice comes from my ancestors. Sometime in the mid-1800s my great-great-grandfather, his wife and their six children were invited, once a year, to have lunch with the director of the company where he worked. My great-great-grandmother, I have been told, always fed her children a hearty soup before they went out. With their stomachs well lined, these charming children never displayed excessive enthusiasm for the elegant and lavishly prepared dishes which were never served to them at home. As a result, my great-great-grandparents acquired the reputation for having extremely well-behaved children.

If you are afraid you will not be able to resist, take my ancestors' advice and eat a couple of hard boiled eggs or a piece of cheese before you leave home. Also, get into the habit of carrying around with you wherever you go, individually wrapped mini-cheeses. Those with cholesterol problems should of course take something like an apple.

These should satisfy your hunger pangs and you can eat as many as you want. As a general rule, whenever you get one of these cravings, you can eat anything from the list of "authorised" foods. Just be sure to avoid lipids after a carbohydrate meal. For instance, you should not eat a piece of cheese at 9 o'clock in the morning if you have just finished a carbohydrate breakfast at 8 o'clock.

In the event that you are invited to a friend's house, your ability to pick and choose is considerably reduced. Let us look at the situation more closely.

Maybe these are old friends or even family. In this case, take advantage of an easy relationship to be frank. Tell them about your new weight-loss method and even enquire before the meal about what is on offer. If your relationship with the cook is particularly close, you might even make a few suggestions!

However, if you are not on particularly close terms with your hosts, you will have to wait until the last minute and improvise from there.

If it is a celebratory meal, you will probably not be served rice, pasta or potatoes as the main part of your meal. So eat the foie gras if it is served, but do not overindulge if you are in Phase One. And do not eat the toast!

If you are served a cheese soufflé, eat along with everyone else, even though it contains flour. But do not aggravate the situation by eating a second or even a third helping.

If you are served a "paté en croute" (a paté in a pastry crust) as a starter, eat only the middle, since it is usually a proteic-lipid, and discreetly leave the rest on your plate. Don't worry, since you are not among intimate friends, no one will point to your dish and say, "hey, you're leaving the best part!" Even were your hostess to notice, she is unlikely to ask you what is wrong with the crust.

For the entrée you should not have too much trouble, and side dishes are usually optional. You can symbolically help yourself to a potato, but no one will be offended if you do not eat it.

Should you still be hungry at this point, you can catch up on the salad and particularly the cheese. If you help yourself to a lot of cheese, your hostess will be appreciative and will certainly excuse you for having left the paté crust.

For a cheeseboard to look attractive, it has to offer a wide selection of cheeses. Unfortunately, it generally remains untouched because at this stage of the meal, the guests have very little appetite left. It is at this point, that you can finally come into your own: by doing justice to the selection of cheeses so carefully prepared by your hostess, you will earn her eternal gratitude!

Dessert is probably the most critical time of the meal. It is always hard to say "no thank you, I cannot eat any more". Insist on a very small portion and, like those who are so full that they cannot eat another bite, leave a substantial part of it on your plate.

Wait as long as possible before you drink anything. And when you do, try to drink red wine – particularly with the cheese.

And then, if the situation has turned out to be worse than anticipated and you manifestly failed to display the imagination required of you to avoid all those bad carbohydrates, if you are still in Phase One, just make certain you are extra careful in following the guidelines of Phase One in future.

Remember that in Phase One, you are still very sensitive to glucose. The whole point of these first few weeks is to raise your tolerance level. If you do not succeed in doing this, you will remain very sensitive.

In fact, the longer you stay in Phase One (which should last at least two or three months), the better are your chances of keeping your weight at its new low level.

On the other hand, if you indulge yourself to excess two or three weeks into Phase One, you risk returning immediately to the weight you were when you began the course. If this happens, you will probably feel completely discouraged. However, you must not despair. Tell yourself as you have in other situations, that losing a battle does not mean that one will therefore lose the war.

DINNER (Phase One)

Dinner should be either proteic-lipidic or carbohydrate based. And by "carbohydrate", I mean of course, "good carbohydrate".

Dinner – Version One

A proteic-lipidic dinner is virtually identical to lunch. The only difference is that your dinners will normally take place at home, where your choices will probably be more limited. However, if you have been able to convince your wife and family to adopt your new eating habits, all should be plain sailing.

The ideal way to start your dinner is with a hearty vegetable soup made from leeks, celery, cabbage, etc. You can use any vegetable as long as it is listed in Table 1 (p.153). Be careful not to add potatoes or carrots. Many soup connoisseurs will tell you that the potato is an essential thickener. This is true, but you can instead also use celery, an egg yolk or even pureed mushrooms.

To bring out the flavour of your soup, you can even put in a knob of butter or a small spoonful of "crème fraîche" – unless of course, you have problems with your cholesterol level.

For your main course, you can eat any type of meat your like – or even better, fish, because it is easier to digest. You may have been told that older people should refrain from eating meat at night, but this advice stems from the fact that it is extremely difficult for the body to expel the toxins derived from meat if carbohydrates have been ingested during the course of the meal. If this happens, the incautious diner is liable to sleep badly and suffer from indigestion.

Besides meat or fish, there are always eggs. Eggs can be prepared in a wide variety of ways. Eat an omelette with a salad. It is a simply delicious combination!

As far as the cheese family is concerned, take advantage of being at home and eat some yoghurt. Yoghurt is an excellent food because it contains elements that reconstitute the intestinal bacteria that aid the digestion process. But be careful! Stay away from yoghurt with artificial flavourings or fruit, and be sure that the lacteal ferment is natural.

If you are eating at home, use that time to enjoy the simple meals you enjoy most. Stew for example. Also, eat what you rarely find in restaurants – things like boiled or steamed artichokes. They are delicious, full of vitamins and minerals, and they contain considerable amounts of fibre that will help intestinal function. Above all, do not forget to eat vegetables: tomatoes, spinach, aubergine, cauliflower, leeks, courgettes, mushrooms, etc.

Dinner – Version Two

This dinner is based on *good carbohydrates.*

Besides the foods that are always forbidden (the bad carbohydrates like sugar and potatoes), in Phase One it is absolutely crucial that you avoid eating protein or lipids with a carbohydrate meal.

No lipids means no meat, no oil, no fish, no butter, no eggs, no cheese, except non-fat cheese like the kind you use at breakfast.

So all we have left are green vegetables, brown rice, beans and lentils. But be careful: no butter, margarine or other animal fats.

We can also add wholewheat pasta to this list but as you will not be eating it with either butter or cheese, I suggest you use the tomato sauce already recommended with brown rice (see Part Two, Chapter 1).

Wholewheat pasta used to be difficult to obtain. Not so anymore – though you do have to read the list of ingredients carefully, to make sure there are no fatty substances in the pasta. The problem these days is more of a gastronomic one: many of the wholewheat pastas taste awful! So if you do have difficulty in finding something you like, a visit to the Montignac Boutique in London[7] may leave you agreeably surprised.

Here to conclude then, is a suggestion for dinner version two:

– *Home-made vegetable soup,*

---

[7] Montignac Boutique, 160 Old Brompton Rd. LONDON SW5 0BA Phone:0171.370.2010, where you will be able to find most of the foods mentioned in this chapter.

— *Brown rice/ Wholewheat pasta with tomato sauce* (unsweetened or home-made),
— *Non-fat cheese.*

Or:

— *Raw vegetables: celery, cucumbers, cauliflower etc.,*
— *Lentils,*
— *Low-fat yoghurt.*

I have given you these examples of a carbohydrate meal in order to be as thorough as possible. However, in Phase One this type of dinner is much more limited than it is in Phase Two, when you can again eat your beans and spaghetti with meat or tomato sauce made with olive oil.

While following Phase One, for nutritional reasons your guiding principle should be to have as many carbohydrate meals as you do protein-lipid meals. During the course of a week, you might have 5 breakfasts with bread and unrefined cereals, and 3 lunches and dinners with beans, vegetables, etc.

SNACK MEALS

It often happens that, for a number of reasons, you simply do not have time to eat a full meal. Usually lunch is the meal that is sacrificed, and to save time you either skip the meal completely or you quickly gulp down a sandwich. Never do this.

Never skip a meal. It is one of the so-called "golden rules" of proper dietary practice. If you like, eat four or five meals a day, but *never* forgo one of the three main meals. It is the biggest mistake you could possibly make and the best way to destabilise your metabolism. Consider it a prohibited practice and advise others against it. If you do eliminate a meal, your body will act like a malnourished dog burying any spare bone or scrap to guard against possible hunger in the future.

At this point, I am sure you no longer even think about those ham and cheese sandwiches from your favourite pub or coffee shop, or those infamous burgers in their little white buns. So what can you eat instead of your usual snack lunch? It simply takes a bit of imagination allied to the knowledge you have already gained.

Anyway, here are a few examples of items you can buy for your snack lunch at the office or on a journey:

- *Ham* (cooked or smoked) is recommended because it always comes in thin slices, so you do not need a knife and fork to eat it.
- *Dry sausage or salami*: You will need a knife, but your Swiss army knife will do the job more than adequately.
- *Hard boiled eggs*: These are easy to find in delicatessen and corner shops.
- *Cheese*: Any cheese will do, but since we must stay in the realm of the practical, you should stay away from gooey and smelly cheeses like brie or camembert; as they may not be entirely appreciated by your neighbours in a train or on a plane. Choose *hard cheeses* like cheddar or gruyere, or individually wrapped ones that come from the continent.
- *Tomatoes* are ideal if you have a supply of tissues nearby. They can be eaten like fruit.
- *Smoked Salmon of Seafood Sticks* are particularly suitable if you have a cholesterol problem.

If you have not eaten anything all day, you can eat a meal consisting only of fruit. Eat until you are satisfied. The only problem is that fruit is rapidly digested. A few hours later, you will probably be hungry again, so just grab another apple.

Even in the most dire situations, never fall back on forbidden carbo-hydrates like biscuits, commercial chocolate containing less than 72% cocoa solids, and particularly those pseudo-chocolate bars consisting almost entirely of sugar and fat.

Conclusion

We have now come to the end of Phase One. If you are used to eating a lot of sugar, or are a dessert fanatic, you should be able to lose at least two kilos – about five pounds – during your first week in Phase One. But do not stop there, because, in two days, you risk putting back on what took you eight days to lose.

After this initial period, weight-loss will occur less spectacularly. However, if you follow the guidelines closely, you should continue to lose weight on a regular basis.

This loss of weight should follow a sustained rhythm though it may well be influenced by individual factors, as has already been mentioned.

It is known from experience that men obtain results more quickly than women, though this may not apply to men who are suffering from symptoms of anxiety or following specific medical treatment, since some medications encourage weight gain.

A woman on the other hand, is more prone to water retention (during her period, under stress, or for emotional reasons), and calculating weight loss is therefore more difficult over a short period of time such as a week. But this does not mean the results will be less satisfactory. Quite the reverse, in fact.

It has been noticed that certain women sometimes have more difficulty than others in obtaining results, and five possible causes have been identified:

- anxiety, which stimulates insulin secretion;
- hormonal imbalances occurring during adolescence or menopause;
- thyroid problems, which are rather rare;
- an initial resistance generated in certain female organisms that have been subjected to repeated aggressive lowcalorie diets in the past.
- the use of medicines such as amphetamines, hypertension drugs and anti-depressants.

If you had some problems with the level of cholesterol in your blood, from now on there should be no cause for anxiety. Once you learn how to manage your consumption of lipids intelligently, this worry should be a think of the past.

Avoid saturated fats which increase bad cholesterol. Instead, choose lipids or fats that will lower bad cholesterol and those that will increase good cholesterol – notably olive oil. These ideas are acknowledged by the major specialists in the world and the scientific publications in this field are impressive (See Part One, Chapter 6 and Technical Appendix).

Although it is highly improbable, it is possible your doctor may not agree with this new approach, because it was not taught at medical school. Remember, in this field as in others, new ideas take time to be generally accepted, despite the irrefutable scientific evidence to back them up.

Today, for example, no one still believes that new-born babies should be wrapped like mummies to keep their limbs from being deformed. However, for hundreds of years, mothers believed it was their duty to swaddle their new-born babies. Only very recently, when respectable members of the medical establishment expressed their disapproval, did this practice cease. Now we shudder to think of the millions of babies that suffered and perhaps died, because their mothers followed these barbarous ill-informed practices.

If you follow the guidelines given to you for Phase One, you will unquestionably lose weight. If you do not, or if weight-loss is unbearably slow, you are probably doing something wrong.

In this case, you should, over a period of time, keep a meticulous list of everything you eat from the time you wake up to the time you go to sleep. If you then refer to this book again, you will then almost certainly discover what is wrong.

You may be eating soups on a regular basis which you have been assured, contain only "authorised" vegetables like tomatoes, sorrel, leeks, etc. Be more suspicious and check what the ingredients actually are. You may discover that your famous soups come in cans or packages. If you read the ingredients on the label you may find that, in addition to the vegetables, the soup also contains bad carbohydrates in the form of starch fillers, sugars, dextrose and other artificial thickeners or additives.

So be suspicious! Even if the principles put forward in this book are not difficult to apply, they require – at least in Phase One – some effort and it must be admitted, some sacrifices. So do not compromise the results by being too trustful.

In addition, it is necessary to bear in mind that one of the results of the method we are implementing, is to force our organism to reactivate one of its original functions, that is to manufacture part of its own glucose from its fat reserves. Formerly, it was quite happy to lazily use up the glucose found in excessive quantities in "bad" carbohydrates.

It is therefore quite possible that when you change your eating habits, your body will be reluctant to start making its own glucose. This can result in sudden bouts of fatigue, particularly at moments of physical activity, when playing some form of sport.

Should this happen, you should bear in mind that this reaction will persist only for a few days

Under no circumstances should you give way to eating "bad" carbo-hydrates, in order to raise the amount of glucose in your bloodstream artificially. During this period, you may however compensate by eating dried figs or black chocolate containing a minimum of 70% cocoa solids, which are good carbohydrates.

DURATION OF PHASE ONE

The natural question to ask when you arrive at the end of this chapter, is: "How long should I continue in Phase One?".

Well, I suppose I could reply by saying that Phase One should last long enough for you to get rid of your excess weight, bearing in mind that the rate of slimming will vary from one individual to the next. But I could also say that the end of Phase One occurs when you reach your ideal weight. To calculate what that should be, I merely have to refer you to page 198.

However, rather than talk of ideal weight, we should rather talk about weight related to shape or a "balanced weight" – a very individual concept related to reaching a threshold beyond which the body decides it will get no thinner.

If you have ten or fifteen kilos to lose (between 22 to 33 pounds) Phase One could last from several weeks to several months. If you only have four or five kilos to lose (between 9 to 11 pounds), you might be tempted to cut short the programme as soon as you have reached your goal weight.

Now I would remind you that in addition to losing weight, the purpose of Phase One is to calm the pancreas and raise its tolerance to glucose.

So, if you prematurely cut short Phase One, you may well have given your pancreas insufficient time to recover its equilibrium.

If on the other hand, you have no weight to lose but are following the method solely to rediscover a greater physical and intellectual vitality, then the problem is evidently the same. You have a vested interest in prolonging Phase One as long as possible – at least a month – in order to stabilise all the metabolic and digestive functions of the body.

In reality, the question of how long Phase One should last scarcely arises, for the transition to Phase Two generally does not happen from one day to the next, but rather over a period of time.

CONCLUDING REMARKS REGARDING PHASE ONE

Phase One, which is essentially concerned with losing weight, rests on one main principle which I have developed in the course of the previous chapters – the principle of choice. That is:

- the choice between "good" and "bad" carbohydrates, which means that only carbohydrates with a low glycaemic index (below 50) may be used to make up a carbohydrate meal;
- the choice of carbohydrates with a very low glycaemic index (below 15) – namely the majority of green vegetables – to accompany meat and fish dishes;
- the choice between "good" and "bad" fats or lipids, which has to be made in our attempt to prevent the onset of cardio-vascular disease.

It should be clear then, that Phase One it is not a question of eliminating carbohydrates or fats from our diet, but simply of selecting those that are beneficial and eliminating those that are damaging to our health.

The regime of Phase One is therefore perfectly balanced in the traditional sense of the term and has the advantage of imposing no restriction with regard to quantity

Let us now summarise the main principles of Phase One.

- *Never mix bad carbohydrates with lipids at the same meal.*
- *Avoid eating carbohydrate-lipids* like milk, chocolate, avocados, liver, hazelnuts, biscuits.
- *Eliminate sugar* completely from your diet.
- *Never eat refined flours.*
- *Only eat bread made from totally unrefined or wholemeal flour* (and eat it only at breakfast).

- *Eliminate potatoes*, especially roasted or fried potatoes.
- *Eliminate white rice.*
- *Never eat pasta made from refined flours.*
- *Eat fruit on its own*, on an empty stomach, and if possible eat the skin.
- Temporarily *give up all alcohol* in all its forms, such a aperitifs, wine, beer, cocktails, liqueurs and spirits.
- *Avoid strong coffee or tea*. Get into the habit of drinking decaffeinated coffee or tea.
- *Never skip a meal*. Eat three regular meals a day, if at all possible.
- Restrict your consumption of "bad" lipids, choosing "good" lipids to prevent cardiovascular disease.
- Try to drink as little water as possible during your meals to avoid diluting the gastric juices. *Never drink just before a meal.*
- *Take your time to eat*. Chew well and avoid getting excited or tense during the course of the meal.
- *Make your own fruit juices*. Do not substitute with industrial fruit juices which contain added sugar.
- *Eliminate all fizzy drinks* particularly those containing sugar.
- Wait three hours after a carbohydrate meal (like breakfast) before you consume any lipids.
- Wait four hours after a lipidic meal before consuming any carbohydrates.
- *Eat lots of fibre*: lettuce, leeks, asparagus, artichokes, aubergine, etc. (See chart in Part One, Chapter 2).
- *Drink plenty of water between meals* – preferably between 1.5 to 2 litres a day.

WARNING: This list is only a summary of some of the main recommendations in the text. In no way should it be regarded as a condensed exposition of the method. Someone who has not read either the preceding or the following chapters, will be unable to apply the principles of the method properly, and will run the risk of evolving a dietary programme that could prove dangerous – particularly with regard to lipid management.

3

Phase Two –
Maintaining your Weight

We have now reached our "cruising diet".

By now, you will have grasped the basic principles and philosophy behind this new way of eating. You will have given up certain "dangerous" foods for ever, and in the last few weeks, you will have adopted remarkable new eating habits. You will have lost the pounds you originally set as your goal and you are now ready to move on to Phase Two.

Unlike Phase One, which had to take place over a limited period of time, Phase Two can last for the rest of your life. I have been in Phase Two for nearly ten years and have not gained a single ounce. Moreover, I deprive myself of nothing.

Phase Two, as the title above indicates, is all about maintaining your weight. It is in this phase that we are really going to learn how to *manage* our diet.

In Phase One, we cut out a number of foods that we labelled "forbidden." In Phase Two, hardly anything will be completely excluded. Certain foods may have to be avoided, but only under specific conditions.

The guiding principles in this Phase will seem less clearly defined, more subtle. But that is the nature of management.

Management is not just the application of rules that have been defined once and for all. It is the art of applying those rules. Any idiot can apply rules, as we are reminded constantly whenever we deal with any large administrative organisation, whether it is public or private. Administration involves rules, more rules, and nothing else but rules. So I am not asking you to administer your diet as you did in Phase One, but just to manage it.

The difference between administrators (in the literal sense of the word) and managers, lies in the subtlety of the art. Whereas the administrative clerk blindly applies the principles, the manager is inspired by them.

Here is what I suggest.

We will review the basic criteria to see how they can be interpreted and applied.

Sugar (Phase 2)

Sugar remains and always will remain a dangerous product. What I told you in Phase One still holds true here. Get into the habit of excluding sugar from your diet. Even if you have forgotten your artificial sweetener, do not give in and say "a little lump of sugar, just this once, can't really upset everything." You can get away with this approach only if you are 100% sure you have not eaten, and will not eat, a single bad carbohydrate all day.

Be strict! No more sugar in your coffee! No more sugar in your plain yoghurt! Either you must learn to use an artificial sweetener or you must do without.

You should learn to think in terms of equivalents. Tell yourself that one cube of sugar is equal to two glasses of champagne or half a bottle of Bordeaux. You choose!

From now on in Phase Two, the rules will allow you much more freedom than you had in Phase One. But never-the-less, in this "management" phase your discretion should remain scrupulously monitored.

You will in fact be forced to eat sugar, since it is found in most desserts. I will teach you how to choose the desserts that contain the least sugar. But, if you decide to yield to your urge to eat a dessert, you cannot then put sugar in your coffee

Be *inflexible* as far as sugar is concerned. It is a poison and you should treat it as such! With other foods you can be more indulgent.

And what about honey? Without a doubt, this question has been burning inside you since the start. Since it is a natural product and therefore unrefined, you might expect me to speak very well of it. Unfortunately, I shall have to disappoint you, because its glycaemic index is a very high 90 – which means of course that it is a "bad" carbohydrate.

Despite this, like you, I long believed that honey contained vast treasures of health in terms of vitamins, minerals and other trace elements. In fact, it contains little else apart from sugars. I have been totally disillusioned on the subject of honey since the day a bee-keeper informed me that all big honey producers provide their bees with an impressive amount of industrial sugar, partly to make up for the lack of flowers (due to deforestation and the use of weedkillers), but also to improve their yield significantly.

Bread (Phase 2)

One of my brothers, like myself, is a great lover of good red wines. When I told him: "Each time you swallow a mouthful of bread, you should abstain from one glass of Bordeaux." he really understood the seriousness of what eating bread during a main meal entails. As ever, it is question of choice!

During breakfast, if you are eating a carbohydrate-based meal, you should continue to eat only completely unrefined wholemeal bread. If, however, after three months you can no longer stand the sight of cottage cheese or fat-free yoghurt, you may switch to a light table margarine or low-fat butter. But do not use astronomical amounts and only use regular butter if you have no other choice – when you are travelling, for example.

The same rules apply to milk. Stay in the habit of drinking only skimmed milk. If none is available, which often occurs when one is travelling, use a moderate amount of cream or whole milk as a substitute.

The carbohydrate breakfast, as described in Phase One, is not very restrictive, so do not abandon it in Phase Two.

From time to time, I am asked to attend business breakfasts in some of the best hotels of Paris. On those occasions, it is well night impossible for me to resist the urge to taste those delicious croissants oozing with butter.

In such instances, at the end of the meal, I automatically take into account how my dietary balance has been upset. In other words, I will usually make a mental note of what I had for breakfast, and eat prudently and sensibly the rest of the day. For example, I will probably refrain from eating chocolate at lunch, or I will do without wine, if possible, at dinner.

You should now understand that the secret of a well-managed diet lies in a healthy and harmonious balance. Your metabolism can only tolerate lipid-carbohydrate combinations to a certain level. Providing you do not exceed this limit, you will happily maintain your weight.

I cannot tell you what this limit is, because it varies from one individual to the next. It depends on their sensitivity to glucose and the way their pancreas reacts. If you have increased your tolerance to glucose significantly after serious application of Phase One, your pancreas will be more in control and secrete just enough insulin to flush out the surplus sugar in the blood stream. But rest assured, you will easily find out this limit on your own by consulting your bathroom scales regularly.

Naturally, like the good manager you are, you should always keep a sharp eye on your weight and monitor it as you would your bank account. As a professional, you know that you can take care of any discrepancy, as long as you catch it in time.

During lunch, at home, at the cafeteria or in a good restaurant, you should always obey the "golden rule": *no white bread with your meal!* If you enjoy oysters, even though they are carbohydrate-lipids, eat three or four more instead of a piece of buttered bread.

I will not reiterate what I said before about the little bite-size rolls that your table companions devour as soon as they sit down for lunch. Those notorious little rolls are to be banned for ever!

Also, do not eat the toast that is served with your smoked salmon. Instead, order fresh marinated salmon with dill. Not only is it delicious, but it is served without the little pieces of toast. So – no temptation!

If you order foie gras, the toast is again officially forbidden. All the more so in fact, because foie gras is a carbohydrate-lipid anyway! This is, in fact, one of the reasons why it is not listed as a permitted foods in Phase One.

When you get used to eating your meals (except breakfast) without bread, you will finally be able to savour the delectable tastes of the fine dishes you are served. This is particularly true of foie gras, which I highly recommend you order in a restaurant, especially if it is fresh. Which brings me to another rule, one that does not have much to do with the purpose of this book, but more with gastronomy in general, and that is: *in restaurants; order what you cannot eat at home.*

Many people with whom I have eaten in restaurants, both Frenchmen and foreigners, surprise me with the unimaginative and conservative selections they make. Whether they are in Paris, New York or Tokyo, their finger inevitably stops at the classic dishes on the menu that are most similar to the foods they are used to eating at home. The maître d'hôtel or waiter has to draw on all the persuasive powers and diplomacy at his disposal in order to persuade them to choose something that does not resemble their normal daily fare.

If your table companions lack as much creativity and imagination in business, I pity their bosses or their share-holders.

Coming back to our bread, since that is what we were originally discussing, I will grant you one concession – and that concerns cheese. If you are lucky enough to find a restaurant that serves wholemeal bread or something similar, I will allow you, as long as you have not upset your balance with any other major discrepancies, the excellent combination of mature goat cheese rolled in ash, warm bread and a glass of your favourite wine.

Starches (Phase 2)

Even in Phase Two, I remain staunchly opposed to potatoes, white rice, white pasta and maize products.

You must have understood in Phase One that these foods, along with white bread, are invariably the cause of your excess weight. Whenever they are mixed with lipids the results are deplorable. Like bread, it is better to avoid them at lunch and dinner.

Unless of course, you deliberately decide otherwise. In which case, bear in mind that there is a way of reducing the negative effects of "bad" carbohydrates. In fact it is true of all carbohydrates, because when they are eaten with fibre, their glycaemic index is lowered.

For example, if you decide to eat chips for the sheer pleasure of it, order an enormous salad to accompany them. The fibre will minimise the dietary imbalance the chips will inevitably create.

Sometimes, you may be caught in situations where it is difficult to avoid introducing the discrepancy into your dietary plan. But try not to give in too quickly. By that I mean, try and *program* yourself to react negatively and not even consider the possibility of deviating from the plan you have set yourself. There will be many occasions when you will fail to keep to your plan, so do your very best to keep those occasions to the minimum.

In "nouvelle cuisine" restaurants, your task will be easier. Each dish is prepared individually. With three of four vegetables served with the dish, if you leave one of them, no one is likely to hold that against you.

But then, you could be invited to dinner by your next-door neighbour or by your "difficult" ageing aunt. If you leave a single noodle or grain of white rice on your plate, socio-family relations are liable to suffer a serious set-back. So allow a further discrepancy in your diet, even if you cannot enjoy any forbidden pleasure by way of compensation.

Remember that when you finish your plateful of carbohydrates – eaten with or without pleasure – you will still have to rule out either your drink or your dessert. If by misfortune, you are not only forced to swallow your rice, but also finish off the suffocating rum-baba your hostess has specially prepared for you, you will have a considerable amount of re-balancing to do. And perhaps, depending on the damage done, you may even have to return to Phase One for a few days, in order to readjust your internal equilibrium.

After these binges, be on guard against a natural tendency to consider everything a lost cause. You must not despair and say: "I might as well give up as the damage has now been done". *This is an ever-present danger which must be resisted at any cost.*

Never abandon your proper eating habits under the pretext that "during the Christmas season it is impossible to apply them anyway."

I know from a long period of experience that even in the most critical situations, it is always possible to manage your diet. You may, of course, upset the balance because of professional or social obligations, but in the longer term you can maintain your equilibrium by rigorously applying your regime in the days that follow.

This does not mean that you can apply my method in a roller-coaster fashion. If you do, you will never get anywhere.

As you will have understood, my method sets out to raise your tolerance level to glucose as high as possible. If you allow your regime to "roller-coaster", coming back to Phase One every time you gain 7 or 8 pounds, you will never achieve this condition.

I can tell you that after ten years in Phase Two, my glucose tolerance level is extremely high. This means that the more vigilant you are in the first few months and first few years, the easier it is to compensate

91

subsequently for any major disruptions to your regular diet.

The method presented to you here aims to "decondition" you or extricate you from the bad eating habits you have followed. since childhood. One of the keys to success rests on positive "reconditioning." If you are able to recondition yourself properly in Phase One, the effort needed will be considerably less in Phase Two. By then you should have acquired a number of natural reflexes that will lead you to make the "right" choices in managing your diet.

If you see fresh pasta on the menu, and if you are tempted to order, then do so. But do so knowing what the effect will be. Relish the pleasure, but make a mental note of the negative effects so you can compensate for them later on.

Let us say that you have decided during the course of a meal, to eat foie gras, oysters and some scallops – without depriving yourself of a Brouilly that goes so well with crustacea – and that around your main dish you come across some potatoes, some rice or even some pasta, *do not touch them at all costs!*

I know you are not completely convinced that you will have the will power to leave on your plate something you really enjoy. Well, you will see that in fact it is be easier than you thought. Because when you reflect on the pleasure derived from the spectacular results you had in Phase One, applying the brakes now will be nothing more than a conditioned reflex.

And so, step by step, you will gradually arrive at a point of self-regulation – or should I say, self-management.

Fruit (Phase 2)

As for fruit, the rules in Phase One will continue to be applied here. You should always eat fruit on an empty stomach.

As we saw earlier, it is not the small amount of carbohydrate (fructose) contained in the fruit that causes the trouble, but whether or not the fruit is mixed with other foods. There are certain fruits however, whose fructose content is so low that they can now be eaten as often as you wish. These, as you have guessed, are strawberries, raspberries and blackberries.

From April to October, you can find raspberries and strawberries in just about every restaurant. If you are allergic to strawberries, keep in mind that there is a nine in ten chance that your allergy is due to secondary effects from the intoxicating effects caused by "bad" carbohydrates. So during the course of Phase One, there is a good chance your allergy will vanish like magic. You will probably be surprised to see a number of other minor afflictions that have bothered you until now, disappear very quickly also.

I will come back to these strange phenomena in another chapter.

At lunch or dinner, in a restaurant or at home, eat strawberries or raspberries.

If your meal has been exclusively proteic-lipidic, you can even add fresh cream to your raspberries or strawberries. However, add no sugar – only an artificial sugar like "Nutra-sweet" if you must!

If you have not created any imbalances in your diet (apart from the wine), you can even ask for Crème Chantilly or vanilla-flavoured whipped cream on your strawberries, even if it does contain a small dose of sugar. If you are at home, make your own whipped cream with an artificial sweetener.

Many readers of the previous edition have written to ask me if cooked fruits are considered to be in the same league as raw fruits. I am tempted to answer yes, but with qualifications.

Cooked fruit ferments less than raw fruit and the gastric perturbation that results is therefore less drastic. Apple sauce, stewed pears or a Peach Melba would therefore represent only a slight discrepancy on this score.

Nevertheless, it is important to emphasise that cooking raises the glycaemic index of fruit by weakening the bonding between fibre and sugar.

As far as canned fruit in syrup is concerned, it should be completely excluded, because of the large amount of sugar added to make the syrup. Uncooked dried fruits have a medium glycaemic index but contain very good fibre. They can be consumed to sustain strong physical exertion. Dried figs are certainly the best choice and dried bananas the worst. Dried fruit in Muesli (marketed as a breakfast cereal in Britain) is allowed. However, no sugar or honey should be added and make certain the cereals are not refined.

Desserts (Phase 2)

This section is very dear to me since I have a sweet tooth and am, by nature, a great lover of desserts at the end of a meal.

Everyone has a few weak spots. You just have to know how to handle them.

Personally, I could do without potatoes for the rest of my life, without fresh pasta for at least a year, but never could I go more than a week without chocolate.

Alongside "nouvelle cuisine", we also have "nouvelle patisserie" and it should be recognised that for more than ten years considerable progress has been made by our great chefs (who are all great "pâtissiers") in terms of creativity and invention,

Perhaps I may be forgiven for claiming that French pastries are currently the best in the world for their originality, their beauty, their natural flavours and above all their lightness. Gaston Lenôtre[1] is undoubtedly one of the great masters of his art and he takes great pleasure from having trained so many disciples who are now close to being his equal.

Even the "Framboisier" chain[2] make desserts that remain unmatched by any other patissier in their category. Their light and original mousses are for me, a constant source of amazement.

Within the framework of our eating method, you will be able to indulge in these delicacies throughout Phase Two. If you love pastries, try to eat only the lightest ones, which are, by the way, the best ones. Those containing the least sugar and flour are most compatible with our eating principles. Just as nouvelle cuisine sauces infrequently contain flour, nouvelle patisserie, especially in the mousses, uses very little sugar, and hardly any flour.

The bitter chocolate fondant (you will find the recipe in the appendix at the end of the book) requires less than two ounces of flour for a two-pound cake, in other words, about 5%. No sugar is added. The small amount of sugar in the chocolate is enough to make this cake an epicurean delicacy; one that will only cause a slight upset in your dietary balance.

[1] Gaston Lenôtre, 44 reu d'Auteuil, Paris 16e.
[2] Framboisier, 11 avenue du Colonel Bonnet, Paris 16e.

I also suggest a chocolate mousse that possesses few carbohydrates except for those in the bitter chocolate. If you do not find the mousse sweet enough, which would surprise me, add a small dose of powdered artificial sweetener (see recipe in appendix).

I began this section on desserts by talking about chocolate, not only because it is one of my greatest passions, but also because, if it is a top quality (rich in cocoa), it will contain very few carbohydrates.

But there are other attractive "nouvelle pâtisserie" desserts to choose from. The bavarois, for example, is a fruit mousse that has the same consistency as a flan. Choose a strawberry or raspberry bavarois if you can. A bavarois does contain sugar and other carbohydrates, but in reasonable amounts. Without getting caught up with percentage calculations, let us just say that your slice of bavarois has fewer carbohydrates than a forkful of chips, a piece of toast or a couple of biscuits.

In addition to the bavarois, there is the charlotte – which I would describe as a sort of bavarois clothed in biscuit. If you are tempted by this cake, eat the mousse interior but leave the biscuit which is of no real gastronomic interest and is also a "bad" carbohydrate.

If you like ice-cream and sorbets, do not hold back. There is usually very little sugar in sorbets, and top rate ice-creams do not contain very much either. However, do remember ice-cream contains lipids.

Contrary to the commonly held belief, the cold of the ice cream does not aid the digestive process. Many people believe it does because of the momentary effects that are triggered by these frozen desserts.

If you are a great ice-cream enthusiast, you will probably prefer your ice-cream covered with a hot chocolate sauce, under a mound of whipped cream, delicately sheltering beneath a Japanese paper umbrella. If so, dig in, because their glycaemic index is a low 35. In terms of upsetting your diet, it will cause less damage than one horrible potato.

As for pies, home-made, upside-down, or prepared any other way, you should stop and think before you order because of the amount of bad carbohydrate contained in the flour. But again, everything is a matter of choice. Your slice of pie is no worse than one baked potato or two spoonfuls of white rice.

If you have not upset your diet all day, then you are free to make your choice. As in any other case, only indulge if you are sure your gratification is worth the sacrifice you are making.

Alcohol (Phase 2)

Alcoholic drinks should be managed in the same way. In Phase Two, as I have said earlier on, you are allowed to reintroduce alcohol into your daily diet in a limited way. Again, you will have to make choices. Do not begin by reintegrating the aperitif, white wine, red wine and the after dinner liqueur all at once (I hope this is not how you used to drink anyway). Even if it is a special meal, which by definition will require you to make other sacrifices, it is hardly possible to drink to that extent. So it is a question of managing our drinking habits in the same way as we do our eating habits.

Aperitifs (Phase 2)

For your aperitif, choose a glass of quality champagne rather that a high proof alcohol such as whisky or gin, even if you add water or tonic[3] to them. The discrepancy will be less serious. The amount of alcohol contained in a glass of whisky is roughly equivalent to half a litre of red wine.

This is why, in restaurants, I never order an aperitif. To trick my table companions, I usually order a glass of wine in the guise of an aperitif. Most of the time however, I simply ask the maitre d'hotel to bring us the bottle of wine we will be enjoying with our meal. A young Bordeaux, a superior Gamay or Beaujolais will go well with just about anything. So, you do not have to wait until everybody has ordered before selecting a wine, and you can always order more wine during the meal, if you like.

Paradoxically, drinking wine as an aperitif is a habit the French have picked up abroad. In New York, Berlin or Singapore, you can order a glass of wine as a cocktail and unlike France, the maitre d'hotel will not raise an eyebrow and think you are just "up from the sticks".

I do not think I need to tell you not to order a second aperitif, especially if it is whisky or anything similar. If you cannot help yourself,

[3] Tonic Water contains sugar, so avoid it.

which would surprise me, you can always order a second glass of champagne.

The aperitif is the hardest part of a meal to get through when you are managing your diet. It can drag on for over an hour, particularly if you are dining at the home of a friend and your hosts are waiting for the last of their guests to arrive.

If you are polite and arrive on time, you may have to spend a couple of hours over your aperitif – which is a very long time if you have only bad carbohydrates to nibble on. Having decided beforehand to save your sacrifices for the excellent wines your host has lovingly allowed to age in his private cellar, dissipating them on snacks you do not much like can be a harrowing experience.

I find Anglo-Saxon parties a particular nightmare. You are invited for 6.30 p.m., and even if you arrive an hour late, do not count on being served food before 9 or 10 o'clock.

I have unhappy memories of one evening at the home of an English family who had just come to live in the outskirts of Paris. At midnight, one French couple got up to leave and were amazed when their hostess said in her charming English accent, "Oh, you're not going, are you? We are just going to eat."

The couple, believing that the British normally eat early, had arrived punctually at 7 o'clock. Four hours later, having accepted only one drink and suffering the full effects of hypoglycaemia, they were on the verge of despair.

At such parties, I am always astonished at the amount of alcohol both hosts and guests are able to drink on an empty stomach. You may also have met the well-intentioned host who perpetually checks to make sure that the glass of his guest is always full. As a result, you can never keep track of how much you have been drinking.

Not that it seems to worry anybody else. Most of the other guests will even make sure they take their aperitif to the table with them when asked to take their seats, especially if the glass still full.

In the United States, there is one particular hazard you have to guard against.

When you enter a restaurant, to get from the door to your table, you are obliged to pass by the bar. Depending on the will power of your friends, your pit-stop here can drag on for hours. And when finally you reach your table, do not think the ordeal is over then because as likely as not, when you sit down you may well be served yet another "final" aperitif.

I have discussed the aperitif at some length, in order to make clear what sort of traps you can get into when you are trying to manage your diet. However, in my experience, you can always get round the problem if you really want to.

In any case, remember that the first rule is to eat something proteic-lipid beforehand – like cheese, cooked meat or fish – because drinking on an empty stomach is not only a heresy, it is also the beginning of a metabolic catastrophe.

Wine (Phase 2)

I have often referred to wine in the previous chapters, and you probably know by now that in general my preference is for red wines, and Bordeaux in particular.

This is not to say that I exclude all white wines or red wines other than Bordeaux from my diet. I enjoy many of the American wines that have, in this last decade, reached high levels of excellence. However, yet again, it is all a matter of choice within the limits you have set yourself.

For example, I will not deny that Sauternes is the best wine to accompany an excellent foie gras. However, good management is also the art of compromise!

Liver, as you now know, is a carbohydrate-lipid. Even though the dietary imbalance it creates is small, it nonetheless exists. Sauternes is a fairly sweet wine and it has the potential to upset the balance of your diet. If you use all your "wild cards" at the beginning of the meal, how then will you "manage" the rest?

Feel free to decide whether or not to drink your Sauternes, but try to keep strictly to the minimum required to enjoy your foie gras to the full, because that one glass of Sauterne is approximately equal to two glasses of Medoc.

Since we can drink more than one glass of wine at dinner without disrupting our carbohydrate-lipid balance, we might as well choose one that will create the least amount of damage. Red wines and dry whites are an advantage in this respect.

However, I must make some distinctions between different red wines. Top of the list are the young red wines with about 9 to 12 degrees of alcohol. These include Beaujolais, Gamay, Loire wines like Chinon, Bourgueil, Anjou or Saumur-Champigny and many other little 'vins de pays' that are drunk when they are young, such as those from Savoie. The further south you go, the higher the degree of alcohol in the wine. But these wines should not be excluded just because of that. Many people believe that a Bordeaux is only good after it has aged a number of years. Not so! And I would like to thank all the wine specialists and editors of gastronomic reviews who have promoted the idea that many Bordeaux can be enjoyed young. For this reason, many good restaurants have now included excellent young Bordeaux on their wine list. Food critics have taken note and are impressed by the quality/price ratio.

This is not to say that we should neglect the fine vintages sleeping away in the cellars. Far from it. But remember, you never drink an aged wine, be it a Bordeaux or a Burgundy: you taste it. As a cultured individual and as a professional, you should never forget this.

Many times, I have noticed with sadness that Frenchmen are shame-lessly uncultured compared to many foreigners, who have proved them-selves impressively adept in wine appreciation. I, for one, have found my knowledge of wines quite helpful in the context of public relations and especially during business meals. Just as a conversation starter or to introduce people from abroad to the speciality of your region, the topic is far more interesting than the weather or the stock market.

I once had an American boss who was the president of a wine-tasting club in Chicago. I can assure you that, whereas everyone else perceived him as an impossible and unapproachable boss, I got on well with him – simply because every time we met, I was able to add something to his knowledge of wines. It is to him I owe a lot of what I know today about wines, because he forced me to update my own knowledge continuously.

However, to get back to my wine suggestions for you in Phase Two, you can enjoy three to four glasses of any red or dry white wine with your meal without upsetting your dietary equilibrium. Here is how you go about it:

- *Fresh marinated salmon*
- *Grilled trout with fennel and ratatouille*
- *Salad*
- *Raspberries and cream*
- *Decaffeinated coffee*

Three glasses of wine during this meal will not cause you to gain a single ounce, so long as you refrain from drinking until after the first course; in other words, after having consciously ingested sufficient food to neutralise the effect of the alcohol. The wine will not even make you feel sleepy, as many believe.

Next time you have a meeting after lunch, pay attention to those who doze off. More likely than not it will be those who have eaten an excessive amount of bad carbohydrate, especially white bread, and, strangely enough, have refused to drink wine. Take advantage of times like these to conduct negotiations. You will definitely come out on top.

Although latest findings indicate that 3–4 glasses of wine during the course of the day, are good for your cardio-vascular system, you can of course abstain from wine if you please. However, the point of this book is to show you how, by following a few basic rules, you can continue to fulfil your professional obligations and eat according to your fancy.

A wise habit I urge you to adopt, however, is to refrain from drinking on an empty stomach.

If you drink on an empty stomach, the alcohol will be absorbed very quickly into your blood stream and bring about the effects with which we are now quite familiar: insulin secretion, creation of fat reserves, and sometimes dizziness.

If the alcohol is mixed with other foods in the stomach, the metabolic process will slow down, and the effects will be less marked.

We can thus conclude that it is better to start drinking as late in the meal as possible, even if you are forced to catch up with your fellow diners at the end.

I also recommend that you never drink water and wine at the same meal. This may seem contradictory, but let me explain.

When you drink wine with your meal, it is metabolised at a slower rate, since the alcohol is absorbed by the other foods. The metabolic process will be even slower if the foods ingested are proteins or lipids (meat, fish), which has important implications if we consider that the slower the digestive process, the less "fattening" it will be.

On the other hand, if you alternate drinking water and wine, you will dilute the alcohol and the other foods will quickly be saturated with the wine and water mixture, leaving a residue to be absorbed straight into the bloodstream as if you had consumed it on an empty stomach.

You have probably been told that water will eliminate the toxins from your body. Even though this is true, water is bad for digestion; it dilutes the gastric juices, and speeds up the metabolism of alcohol.

So, drink as little as possible while you are eating, and never mix water with wine. But drink water between meals.

After-Dinner Drinks (Phase 2)

Since I told you that alcohol is metabolised more efficiently if taken at the end of a meal, you may expect me to say that an after-dinner drink will do less harm than a glass of non-sparkling mineral water.

The small after dinner drink may perhaps assist the process of digestion, since alcohol helps dissolve fats. Hence the name digestif. If your meal has been rich in fats, the alcohol may therefore assist in the digestive process.

My grandmother (originally from Bordeaux), who quietly passed away at the ripe old age of 102, religiously ended each meal with a glass of a famous liqueur. Moreover, when she was at the table, she never drank anything else but Bordeaux. Personally, I have never seen her drink a glass of water during the course of a meal.

My other grandmother, from the region of Armagnac[4], died much younger at the age of 99. She also had her little drop of something at the end of her meal, though not regularly.

I would not go so far as to say that they both found the recipe for their longevity in their little after-dinner drinks, but you must admit there are some troubling aspects to the story.

[4] Armagnac is a type of brandy produced in the department of Gers, which in France is almost as famous as Cognac.

Technically, I would say that if the meal has been accompanied by only a little wine, a small quantity of spirit at the end cannot have any catastrophic effects.

However, should you decide to drink a glass of cognac that rivals the size of your swimming pool, I would prefer not to be held responsible for the results – particularly if you have also consumed four or five glasses of wine during the course of your meal.

Take into account that a generous glass of spirit is equivalent to about three or four glasses of wine and I will leave you to draw your own conclusions.

Coffee (Phase 2)

In Phase Two, I recommend you stick to the habits you adopted in Phase One. Drink only decaffeinated coffee.

As you will now have brought your bouts of tiredness due to hypoglycaemia under control, the craving for caffeine will have disappeared completely. You might therefore care to know that giving up caffeine is as healthy as giving up nicotine.

As you succeed in raising the tolerance threshold at which insulin is secreted, consuming a little caffeine will not dramatically harm your rediscovered equilibrium.

Other drinks (Phase 2)

All other alcoholic drinks, soft drinks, milk and fruit juices, have been covered in Phase One. I have nothing more to add. Observe these same rules in Phase Two.

Conclusion (Phase 2)

Phase Two is both easier and more difficult than the previous phase. It is easier, because there are very few restrictions, and nothing is absolutely forbidden: but it is more difficult, because it requires an informed and subtle management of your diet which must be strictly adhered to. So be vigilant and always on the look-out for ways of avoiding the pitfalls.

The first of these pitfalls is management error. Management error consists of taking account only of one factor at a time when managing your diet. For example, say you drink a glass of whisky before your meal, and then wait for your main course before starting to drink the first of four glasses of wine that you have allowed yourself. Even though you have remembered that the effects of alcohol are lessened when your stomach is full, do not expect any spectacular results if you have taken an aperitif on an empty stomach.

At the end of this chapter I have summarised some of the rules of Phase Two. Learn them thoroughly, in order to apply them harmoniously and efficiently.

However, the biggest pitfall is that of managing your diet like a yo-yo; alternating "letting everything go" with a stringent return to Phase One to save the situation. If you start applying this roller-coaster method, I can assure you that in less than three months you will give up completely and end up where you started, tired and overweight.

The objective you have set yourself (and this is what this book is about), is to reach and maintain a stable weight. You will achieve this goal only through proper management of your diet in Phase Two, which should last you for the rest of your life. Even if Phase Two seems restrictive at first, you will see that every day it becomes a little easier. You will see that gradually your dietary principles will become one with your natural habits and reflexes and you will have successfully conditioned yourself to a new eating philosophy and way of life.

Do not let yourself be influenced or discouraged by those around you who may try to interfere. But by the same token, do not try to change the ways of those who do not want to change. I made the big mistake of wanting to "convert" everyone to my new found "religion" as soon as I had seen the light.

Just concentrate on yourself. Manage your diet without having to tell your table companions about your new found weight-loss method. Even if they make dreadful mistakes in front of you and intuitively you want to make some comment, do not say anything if they have not asked for your advice. You run the risk of putting them on the defensive and just making them feel guilty. Many of them know they are not eating properly but they also feel they do not have the willpower to get out of their rut.

I have already said that although you have a lot more freedom in Phase Two, you need to watch yourself closely. Never be a slave to your weight, but be on guard by keeping a watchful eye on your scales. Your scales should be sensitive enough to reveal whether and by how much you have upset your dietary balance. Little by little, through trial and error, you will get used to knowing how to maintain your ideal weight. And if one unfortunate day, you should find you have strayed from the path you are following, make the necessary corrections to your diet and you will be happily back on course. You will find that little by little you will go over to "automatic plot" without even realising it is happening.

Let us now summarise the main principles of Phase Two.

- *Continue to avoid mixing bad carbohydrates with lipids.* If you are forced to do so, try to consume only a minimum and with as much fibre as possible (a salad, for example).
- *Never eat sugar cubes, powdered sugar honey, jams or sweets. Persist in using an artificial sweetener if you find it necessary.*
- *Eat starches very rarely or not at all* (with the exception of brown rice, wholewheat pasta and dried vegetables such as lentils and beans).
- *Continue eating bread only at breakfast.* Eat only wholemeal bread or bread made from totally unrefined flour.
- *Beware of sauces.* Make sure they do not contain flour or sugar.
- Whenever possible, *use sunflower margarine or fat-free yoghurt instead of butter*, especially at breakfast.
- *Drink only skimmed milk.*
- *Eat plenty of fish and choose "good" lipids to prevent cardiovascular diseases.*
- *Be careful of desserts made with flour.* Eat only strawberries, raspberries and blackberries. In moderation, you can eat chocolate with cocoa solids in excess of 70%, sorbets, ice cream and whipped cream.

  Avoid pastries made from flour and sugar, unless you have eaten no other carbohydrates during your meal. Try to order mousses made only from fruit and eggs, or artificially sweetened puddings.
- *Try to drink as little as possible while you eat.*
- *Never drink alcohol on an empty stomach.*
- *Avoid aperitifs and after-dinner drinks.* Drink them only rarely.
- *Drink champagne or wine as an aperitif* but first nibble something, such as cheese or cooked meats.
- *During your meal, drink either water* (non-sparkling) *or wine* (no more than half a litre a day).
- *Do not drink water if you are drinking wine.*
- *Drink water between meals* (a litre and a half a day).

- *Wait until your stomach is partially full before you start drinking your wine.*
- *Never drink any type of soft drink.*
- *Drink only decaffeinated coffee, or weak coffee or tea.*
- *Distribute your dietary "imbalances" evenly over the course of several meals.*

PART THREE

Food for Thought

1

Hypoglycaemia the Disease of the Century

We have already seen that the metabolism is the process whereby ingested foods are converted into the vital elements needed for a healthy body. When, for example, we speak of the metabolism of lipids, we are referring to the conversion of fats. We have touched briefly on the metabolism of lipids, but in this book we are principally concerned with the metabolism of carbohydrates and its consequences.

We have seen in previous chapters how insulin (a hormone secreted by the pancreas) plays a vital role in the metabolism of carbohydrates. The basic function of this hormone is to act on glucose in the blood to enable it to pass into the cells of the body, and to ensure that it is then converted into glycogen. Glycogen will then be held in the muscles and liver as a reserve of energy for future use. If it is left unused for too long, it will eventually be converted into reserves of fat.

In doing this the insulin chases the glucose (sugar) out of the blood stream, thus reducing the amount of sugar in the blood. If the quantity of insulin produced by the pancreas is too high and is secreted too often – so that there is more insulin in the blood than is required to help metabolise the glucose there – the level of sugar in the blood will fall to an abnormally low level, putting the body into a state of hypoglycaemia.

Contrary to popular belief, hypoglycaemia stems not from a deficiency of sugar, but rather from an excessive secretion of insulin (hyperinsulinism) resulting from a previous sugar binge.

Not only is insulin responsible for the storage of fats, but this hormone also hampers the ability of the organs in the body (especially the liver) to replenish the amount of sugar in the blood, when there is a deficiency. For example, if at around 11 o'clock in the morning you are feeling tired, it is highly probable that your sugar level is below average and you are in a state of hypoglycaemia.

If you consume a carbohydrate – a biscuit or any other sweet snack –

it will rapidly be broken down into glucose. The presence of glucose in your blood will raise the sugar level, and you will feel invigorated. However, the presence of the glucose in your blood will trigger the secretion of more insulin that will in turn lower your sugar level even more than before. Once again, you will be in a state of hypoglycaemia. It is a vicious circle that leads to an addictive behaviour pattern.

Many scientists have explained alcoholism as a consequence of chronic hypoglycaemia. As soon as the alcoholic feels his sugar level dropping, he feels depressed and needs a drink. Alcohol metabolises very quickly into glucose, thereby raising the sugar level. The alcoholic now experiences a sudden feeling of well-being. Unfortunately this will last only a short while, because the insulin secreted in response to the increased presence of sugar will cause the sugar level in the blood to drop even more.

Not long after his first drink, the alcoholic will feel an even stronger urge for yet another, as his body attempts to overcome the unbearable effects of hypoglycaemia. And so the dreadful cycle goes on and on.

The symptoms of hypoglycaemia are as follows:

- fatigue, sudden exhaustion
- irritability
- nervousness
- aggressiveness
- impatience
- anxiety
- yawning, loss of concentration
- headaches
- excessive perspiration, sweaty palms
- feeling chilly
- impotence
- digestive problems
- insomnia
- neuropsychiatric disorders, depression, etc.
- nausea
- difficulty in expressing oneself clearly

The list is not exhaustive but it is quite impressive. If one suffers from hypoglycaemia, all these symptoms will not necessarily manifest themselves, nor are they permanent. In fact, some symptoms are only very briefly apparent and may well disappear as soon as food is consumed. You may have noticed that many people become progressively nervous, unstable, even aggressive as their regular meal time approaches.

One symptom is more common than others, and you may have guessed already which one it is: fatigue.

Widespread fatigue is, in fact, characteristic of the age we live in.

The people who are the most tired tend to be, as you may have noticed, those who sleep the most, who have the most free time and who take the most holidays. In the morning when they get up, they already feel shattered. By the end of the morning they can barely stand. By early afternoon, you will find them snoozing away at their desk, as they are hit by the after-lunch slump. By the end of the afternoon, they are summoning up what remains of their strength to pick up their things and literally drag themselves back home. In the evening they doze off in front of the television set and when it is time to go to bed, they cannot get to sleep. Before they know it, the alarm goes off, and yet another day begins.

They blame their perpetual exhaustion on the stress, the noise and the pollution of modern times, and to fight against this incessant fatigue, they drink a lot of coffee, swallow boxes full of vitamin pills, or take up yoga. What they do not know, is that fatigue is more often than not a problem caused by hypoglycaemia and an unbalanced diet.

These days, the blood sugar level of the average person is abnormally low and it is normally the direct result of a disproportionate amount of bad carbohydrates in the average diet. Too much sugar, white bread, pasta and rice and too many potatoes and soft drinks will inevitably result in an overabundant secretion of insulin.

For a long time, it was believed that only people who were prone to obesity could be hypoglycaemic. Recent studies, mostly conducted in the United States during the last ten years, have shown that many thin people are also victims of a low blood sugar level caused by the excessive amounts of bad carbohydrate they consume. It is true that some people tend to gain weight while others do not because of a difference in their metabolism, but the consequences of a low blood sugar level are the same for all.

These studies have also shown that women are particularly sensitive to variations in their blood sugar levels, a factor that some think may explain their frequent mood shifts. Whether or not this is true, it has been shown that post natal depression is the direct consequence of low sugar levels in the mother's blood after she has given birth.

If you apply the method presented to you in the previous chapter seriously, you will find that besides losing weight, you will also rediscover a renewed vitality, optimism and "joie de vivre". You will sleep better, you will wake up refreshed and you will feel well. You will also feel more positive and dynamic, and you will be able to concentrate better − benefits which will be reflected in your business and personal life.

When you eliminate sugar from your diet and limit your consumption of bad carbohydrates, your pancreas will stop secreting excessive amounts of insulin and the sugar in your blood will stabilise itself at a normal level. When sugar is no longer ingested and only a moderate amount of glucose is metabolised, the body will eventually rediscover its natural instincts which are to produce the glucose it needs from stored fats. An optimum blood sugar level will be attained only under these conditions.

According to the scientists and doctors I have worked with, hypoglycaemia is rarely detected since the symptoms are so numerous and varied, the general practitioner tends to ignore the condition. One of the reasons for this would appear to be a lack of knowledge about the subject, as it appears that only a few hours are devoted to hypoglycaemia in medical school. Moreover, it has always been officially considered that hypoglycaemia should be diagnosed when the blood sugar level falls below 0.45 g/l, when the normal level is between 0.9 g/l to 1.0 g/l. According to specialists in the field, the symptoms associated with hypoglycaemia occur when the sugar level is only slightly below the normal level.

However, the best way of finding out whether you are hypoglycaemic or not, is to apply the principles set out in the previous chapter. If you *are* hypoglycaemic, you will start to notice an improvement in your physical and mental condition in less than a week − an improvement which may take up to a year to be fully realised, depending on your state of health and the length of time you had been hypoglycaemic before you adopted the method.

When finally you achieve a stable sugar metabolism, you will discover a feeling of well-being you never realised existed.

2

Vitamins and Minerals

The modern diet is deficient or at least poor in certain essential nutrients: these are vitamins and minerals, the latter normally being classified as major elements and trace elements. Not only are these substances removed during the refining of foodstuffs, but they tend to be lost in the course of most industrial processes, whether in the production of food or in its conservation.

The consequences of being totally deprived of these nutrients have long been understood. But all the time we are learning more and more about the ill effects caused by relative deficiencies. Two that are worthy of note from our point of view, are fatigue and difficulty in losing weight.

Vitamins

The very word "vitamin" immediately conjures up images of vitality and life.

It is a fact that none of the chemical processes which take place inside us, could happen without vitamins. They play a role in the functioning of the hundreds of enzymes which act as biochemical catalysis within the cells of our bodies.

You might logically suppose that in Western countries, where there are no food shortages, we would never be short of vitamins.

Yet currently that is precisely what is happening as far as the majority of the population is concerned.

Quite apart from those on low-calorie diets who cannot extract the nutrients that they need from the limited range of foods they are allowed, the rest of the population also suffers deficiencies through poor eating habits.

It is well known that high concentrations of vitamins are found in fruit and fibre. But, according to statistics compiled by Professor Cloarec,

37% of people in France never eat fresh fruit, while 32% never eat fresh green vegetables.

The situation is all the more critical because these individuals are the very people who also choose to eat highly refined products, such as white flour and white rice, from which, by definition, the vitamins have been removed.

And yet vitamins are essential for the proper functioning of the human body, even though they are needed in extremely small doses.

However, as the body is not capable of synthesising vitamins – that is, manufacturing them for itself – and it has to extract them from the daily food intake.

Vitamins are of two main types:

1. Water-soluble vitamins, which cannot be stored in the body. These are vitamins B and C and niacin, which leach into the water used for cooking and are lost because the water is not reused to make soup as it was in the old days.
2. Fat-soluble vitamins, which can be stored. In particular, these include vitamins A, D, E and K.

Vitamin shortages

Changes in Western society and the population growth after the Second World War, brought with them the phenomena of urbanisation and rural depopulation.

Hand in hand with the necessity of producing more food came the necessity of producing different food, since for the first time in human history, the place where food was consumed and the place where it was produced were no longer one and the same.

And so, to boost production levels, intensive farming methods were developed, making use of chemical fertilisers, to say nothing of pesticides, insecticides, herbicides and fungicides.

To overcome the problem created by the time it takes to transport foodstuffs to the place of consumption, new conservation techniques were also developed, leading to the general use of additives, chemical preserving agents and irradiation.

All these measures not only contributed to soils becoming progressively depleted, but also led to the foods produced being too full of undesirable chemicals.

This is why we find that even before they are harvested, fruit, vegetables and cereals are considerably impoverished in terms of vitamins, trace elements and other mineral salts.

It is a sobering thought, that levels of vitamins A, B1, B2, B3 and C have fallen by over 30 % in certain vegetables because of the way they are grown.

For example, vitamin E has virtually disappeared from lettuce, peas, apples and parsley, just as there is no longer any niacin in strawberries.

As between one crop of spinach and another, variations in vitamin content ranging from 3mg to 150mg per 100g have been recorded.

The nineteenth century fashion for white bread led to research into the refining of flours. The nutritional death-knell for flour was rung in 1875, with the invention of the steel roller mill. Through systematic industrial refining, bread was to be depleted of the greater part of its nutrients: fibre, protein, essential fatty acids, vitamins, minerals and trace elements.

Devoid of all its vital components because of excessive milling, wheat grain has been reduced to hardly more than pure starch, which has nothing more to offer nutritionally than its energy value.

On the other hand, the vitamin content of some foods can be increased by causing seeds to sprout before they are used.

The deterioration of vitamins in cooking

In fruit and vegetables, substantial losses of vitamin C can occur through oxidation if they are stored for too long, or through cooking.

The greatest losses during cooking result from long, slow cooking at low temperatures. A short cooking time at high temperature will lead to lower loss. This means that vitamins are better conserved by the use of a pressure cooker than using a dish which is left to simmer for hours.

Vitamin deficiency through inadequate diet

If insufficient food is ingested, as inevitably happens in a low-calorie diet, a vitamin deficiency results.

1500 CALORIE DIET	
Vitamins	Percentage of recommended intake
A	30%
E	60%
B1	40%
B2	48%
B6	49%
C	45%
Niacin	43%
B5	40%
B9	38

How to avoid vitamin loss

- Use the freshest produce you can get, rather than foods which have been on the shelves for days.
- If possible, buy your vegetables on a daily basis, in the market or from your local greengrocer.
- Use as little water as possible in preparation (washing, soaking).
- Choose to eat fruits and vegetables raw (except where this causes indigestion).
- Peel fruit and vegetables as little as possible and make only sparing use of the grater.
- Avoid long, slow cooking.
- Avoid keeping food warm for too long.
- Keep cooking water to use in soup; it contains water-soluble vitamins.
- It is preferable to cook vegetables in steam rather than water.
- Organise your cooking so as to avoid having left-overs to refrigerate and heat up.
- Choose quality over quantity, selecting organically grown items where possible.

- Roasting or grilling meat retains the most vitamins.
- Frozen foods are richer in vitamins than tinned ones.
- Keep milk away from light.

Minerals: major elements and trace elements

The human body is continuously subject to a large number of chemical reactions. These could not take place without the presence of minerals, both major and trace elements, which act indirectly through enzymes.

For example, the transmission of nerve impulses depends upon the presence of sodium and potassium. Muscle contraction could not take place without calcium, and the thyroid gland could not produce its hormones without iodine. Similarly, oxygen could not be carried in the blood in the absence of iron, and glucose could not be properly assimilated without chromium.

These micronutrients can be placed in two categories:

1. Major elements such as calcium, potassium, sodium and sulphur.
2. Trace elements, such as chromium, cobalt, zinc, copper, and selenium, which need to be present in extremely small quantities.

A shortage of major elements or trace elements can have a slowing-down effect on the body. It is known, for example, that:

- a manganese deficiency can result in a tendency to hypoglycaemia
- a deficiency of nickel, chromium or zinc prolongs insulin resistance.

You might think that a deficiency in micronutrients arising from poor eating habits could easily be compensated for by taking supplements in tablet or capsule form. The trouble is that, even though these synthetic products can be of help in cases of serious deficiency, they are not easily absorbed by the intestine.

It is therefore better to aim for a normal, varied diet, containing such quantities of all the major and trace elements as the body may need.

This is why the consumption of fruit, vegetables, raw foods, pulses and whole grains is to be encouraged.

The only supplement worth advocating is a daily intake of brewer's yeast and wheatgerm, as these contain nutrients not easily found elsewhere in our modern diet.

Moreover, brewer's yeast is rich in chromium, which helps raise glucose tolerance, in turn resulting in lower blood glucose and a lower level of blood insulin.

3

Sugar is Poison

Sugar is poison! The damage it has done in the twentieth century is as serious as the effects of alcohol and tobacco put together. It is a fact that is well-known. Wherever there is a conference of paediatricians, cardiologists, psychiatrists or dentists, the dangers associated with sugar are acknowledged – as are the dangers of a level of sugar consumption which is rocketing.

In Antiquity sugar was largely unknown. The Ancient Greeks did not even have a word for it.

Around 325 BC, Alexander the Great, who had pushed his world conquest to the plains of the Indus, described sugar as "a type of honey that is found in canes and reeds and grows by the water."

Pliny the Elder, in the first century AD, also refers to sugar as "honey from the cane."

It was not until the time of Nero that the word "saccharum" was invented to refer to this exotic product.

In the seventh century AD, cane sugar appeared in Persia and Sicily, and little by little the Arab countries acquired a taste for it.

Doctor Rauwolf, a German scholar, noted the following in his diary in 1573: "The Turks and the Moors are no longer the intrepid soldiers they were in the times before they discovered sugar."

It was as a result of the Crusades that cane sugar became known in Western Europe. And not long after this time that sugar also began to be cultivated in the southern part of the Iberian peninsula.

The conquest of the New World and the three-way trade that ensued, led sugar to become economically important. Spain, Portugal and England made fortunes trading raw materials for slaves in order to cultivate sugar for importation into Europe. By 1700, France had already built a number of refineries.

His defeat at Trafalgar in 1805 and the continental blockade that resulted, led Napoleon, against the recommendations of his scientists, to develop a way of producing sugar from beet. This became possible only after Benjamin Delessert discovered the extraction procedure in 1812.

By the middle of the 19th century, there was a surplus of sugar in France, even though the level of sugar consumption was very far from what it is today.

In 1880, the average consumption of sugar in Europe per capita was approximately 8 kg[1] a year – which is about equal to ten sugar cubes per day. Twenty years later, in 1900, the rate had more than doubled to 17 kg a year. In 1960, Europeans were consuming 30 kg of sugar a year per head, and in 1972 this had increased to 38 kg.

Within the space of two centuries, Europeans had increased their average yearly sugar consumption from less than one kilo to over 38 per capita.

In 3 million years, it is unlikely mankind has ever made such a drastic change in its eating habits.

And Europeans are far from being the worst affected. The situation is even more dramatic in the United States, where the average person consumes over 63 kg of sugar a year, with Britain not very far behind, with an annual consumption of 45 kg per head.

It is even more distressing to note that the amount of "hidden sugar[2]" represented in these statistics, continues to rise more rapidly. In 1977, the amount of sugar indirectly absorbed (in drinks, desserts, preserves, etc.) was 58% of total sugar consumption. In 1985, it had leapt to 63%.

The figures disguise certain facts. With the introduction of artificial sweeteners and with constant warnings from the medical profession, the direct intake of sugar (in granulated or lump form) is tending to level out or even decrease.

However, the amount of sugar consumed indirectly per capita is alarming. The increase in "hidden sugars" particularly affects children and adolescents. A 150 ml glass of lemonade is equal to five sugar cubes. Moreover, the coldness of the drink conceals its sweetness.

[1] About 100 years earlier, in 1789, consumption was less than 1 kg per person
[2] "Hidden sugar" is sugar that is added to food and drink sold commercially.

Soft drinks are now an integral part of the human diet. The companies that manufacture them are powerful multinationals and the impact of their advertising campaigns is simply phenomenal. It is horrifying to think that they have been able to established themselves in Third World countries, where even the primary nutritional requirements of the population are not guaranteed.

Ice-cream and other frozen desserts which were once bought only on special occasions, are now a permanent feature of our diet thanks to the universal freezer. Vending machines, selling sweets and soft drinks, have been set up in all public places acting as a constant temptation to the consumer. The appeal to the potential consumer is continuous and unrelenting. To resist amounts almost to an act of heroism.

It has become a commonplace to say that sugar is responsible for a large number of ailments. All the world seems to know this fact, yet we make no attempt to change our eating habits, much less those of our children.

Sugar is the principal cause of cardiovascular disease. Doctor Yudkin notes that the Massai and Samburu tribes in East Africa eat a diet rich in fats but practically free of sugar. The amount of coronary illness in these tribes is close to zero. But the natives of the Island of Saint-Helena, who eat a lot of sugar and not many fats, suffer from a significant amount of coronary illness.

Dental caries, caused by the consumption of too much sugar, is so widespread in Western countries that the World Health Organisation puts dental and oral diseases as the third most important disease afflicting industrialised countries, after cardiovascular disease and cancer.

In associating sugar with disease, it is natural to think of diabetes. However, we are mistaken if we believe that diabetes only affects those with hereditary abnormalities. It can also be caused by obesity and obesity in its turn, is normally brought about by an excessive consumption of sugar.

Studies have shown that an excessive consumption of sugar is also responsible for a number of mental illnesses.

In the light of what has been said in previous chapters, you will now understand how sugar can cause hypoglycaemia, disturbing the metabolism and causing many digestive disorders.

Finally, to complete this black list, it must be added that sugar can also lead to vitamin B deficiency. Large amounts of vitamin B are necessary for the assimilation of carbohydrates. Since sugar, like refined starches (flour, rice, etc.), contains no vitamin B, the body is forced to draw on its own vitamin B reserves, leading to a deficiency which can result in neurasthenia (nervous exhaustion), fatigue, depression, and difficulties with concentration, memory and perception.

It is an area that should be explored more often with children who are having learning difficulties at school.

ARTIFICIAL SWEETENERS

I have advised you to eliminate sugar from your diet completely.

Of course, this is an impossible task if sugar is hidden, as it is in desserts. However, you are already taking a big step in the right direction if you stop using granulated and cube sugar. To do this, you have two options: either do without, or replace sugar with an artificial sweetener.

There are four major types of artificial sweeteners. None, except the polyols, has any energy value: so none, except the polyols, has any nutritional value.

Saccharine

Saccharine, discovered in 1879, is the oldest sugar substitute. It is not assimilated by the human system and is 350 times sweeter than sucrose in natural sugar. It sometimes has the advantage of being very stable in an acidic medium and of tolerating average temperatures. Saccharine was the most widely available sweetener until the discovery of aspartame.

Cyclamates

Although their discovery dates back to 1937, cyclamates are less well known. They are made from benzene, are not as sweet as saccharine, and are sometimes accused of leaving an unpleasant after-taste.

The advantage of cyclamates is that they are completely thermostable; that is to say, they will stand up to very high temperatures. The most commonly used is sodium cyclamate, but there are others, including calcium cyclamate and cyclamic acid.

Aspartame

Aspartame was discovered by in 1965 in Chicago by James Schlatter, a research scientist working for Searle Laboratories.

This sugar substitute is the product of two natural amino acids: aspartic acid and phenylalanine. It is 180 to 200 times sweeter than sucrose. It has no bitter aftertaste and taste tests have concluded that it does not have an "artificial" flavour.

Over 60 different countries use it in the manufacture of foods and beverages.

Artificial sweeteners have been a controversial topic for many years. Saccharine was suspected for a long time, of being a carcinogen. However, it does not seem to present any danger if consumed at a rate of under 2.5 mg per kilogram of bodyweight, which would correspond to 60 to 80 kilograms of sugar for an adult of average weight. Some countries though, like Canada, have banned its use.

Cyclamates have also been suspected of being carcinogenic, and were banned in 1969 in the United States.

Since its release, aspartame has been the subject of considerable controversy, though all the studies have shown that it is not toxic, even when administered in large doses, and its use has been endorsed by the United States Food and Drugs Administration.

After undergoing tests for 15 years in the United States, aspartame was finally marketed under the name of "Nutrasweet" in two forms:

- in tablets which dissolve rapidly in hot and cold drinks,
- in powder form, which is particularly suitable for use in desserts and cooking.

In tablet form, it has the same sweetening power as one 5 gm cube of sugar and has 0.07gm of absorbable carbohydrate. In powdered form, one teaspoon of "Nutrasweet" is equivalent to one teaspoon of sugar and contains 0.5 gm of absorbable carbohydrate.

In 1980, the accepted daily dose recommended by the World Health Organisation was 2 tablets per day per kilogram of body weight. In other words, a person weighing eight and a half stone could consume up to 119 tablets in one day without noting any long-term toxic effects. This dose was confirmed in 1984 and 1987 by the Scientific Committee on Human Diet, the European Union equivalent of the FDA in the United States.

However, artificial sweeteners should only be used as a temporary measure, to help wean you away from sugar. Although they have been shown to have no toxic effects, it is thought they could in the long term disturb your metabolism.

Polyols

Within the range of "false sugars", we can also include polyols, or bulk sweeteners, which provide the necessary bulk in certain manufactured products, such as chocolate, chewing-gum and sweets. It is needed because only a very small volume of the artificial sweeteners mentioned above need to be used to give the required degree of sweetness.

Unfortunately, the only advantage of polyols over sugar is that they do not encourage tooth decay. They have almost the same energy value as sugar and release fatty acids to be absorbed in the colon. Their glycaemic index varies from 25 to 65. Because they can ferment in the colon, they can also lead to bloating and diarrhoea.

This means that, contrary to what we are often told, the use of these substances cannot prevent you putting on weight, even less can they help you slim.

The words "contains no sugar" on a label often disguises the presence of polyols, like sorbitol, mannitol, xylitol, maltitol, lactitol, as well as lycasin and polydextrose.

4

The Miracle of Wine

"Wine is a professor of taste.
By teaching us inner awareness,
wine liberates the mind and
enlightens the spirit."

Paul Claudel

Wine is no ordinary drink or a mere thirst quencher.

Since the beginning of civilisation man has attributed mystical qualities to wine. Credited with a "soul" and with physiological and organoleptic properties, it was described by the nineteenth-century writer Huysmans as a "sacramental substance".

From time immemorial wine has had symbolic significance. The moment Noah and his companions set foot on earth after the Great Flood, they planted a vine to celebrate a new beginning. In Greek mythology, Dionysus[1] links wine with joy, happiness and lifting up of the spirit. The spiritual character of wine is so strong, it is no surprise that Jesus himself chose wine to symbolise his blood in the Christian liturgy.

Despite those today who merely see wine as an alcoholic drink, wine has retained much of the noble character that has made it the symbol of celebration over the centuries.

Recent scientific discoveries have brought to light various therapeutic properties of wine well known to our ancestors, which hopefully the doctors of tomorrow will learn about in medical school. For as Baudelaire said, "if the human race were to cease producing wine, the void in human health and spirit that would result, would far outweigh the sum of the excesses for which it has been blamed."

---

[1] Dionysus or Bacchus, the son of Zeus and Semele, was the Greek god of wine, the Liber Pater of the Romans.

AN ANCIENT FORM OF THERAPY

Plato for whom wine was "milk for old men", recommended its use for maintaining good health. To the Greeks, wine was the symbol of humanity and the guarantor of Wisdom.

The doctors of Ancient Egypt were already making use of the medicinal properties of wine some three thousand years before the birth of Christ.

However, it was with Hippocrates – the father of modern medicine – that wine acquired its full credentials as a therapeutic agent. When modern doctors take their oath, they should enshrine in their hearts, this affirmation of their master: "Wine is highly suitable for man if, in sickness and in health, he takes care to drink it with purpose and in proper measure, according to his individual condition."

Hippocrates, who was not without a sense of humour, claimed that sadness and an austere life were the cause of illness. In these instances, he recommended drinking wine to "dilate the spleen and restore good humour".

Saint Paul, Apostle to the Gentiles, in his letter to Timothy in Ephesus, told him with customary authority: "Stop drinking nothing but water; take a little wine for your digestion, for your frequent ailments."

In 79 AD, Pliny the Elder, who was somewhat of a naturalist, observed that "wine, in itself, is a remedy: it nourishes the blood of man and alleviates his worries and sorrows."

It is thanks to the Benedictine monasteries that wine making survived through the Middle Ages. There are some well known remnants of their vineyards still in existence in the region of Burgundy. Saint Benedict, the founder of the order, laid down in his rule that his monks should drink the equivalent of a couple of glasses of wine at every meal, in order to stay alert and to avoid digestive troubles.

During the Renaissance, wine enjoyed a pre-eminent position among the medicines available at the time.

Rabelais[2], a doctor from the region of Chinon and Bourgueil, wrote that "the juice of the vine clears the spirit, heightens understanding, appeases anger, makes sadness flee and brings joy and jubilation."

[2] François Rabelais: a 16th century French author who wrote the tales of Gargantua

According to Montaigne, the 16th century philosopher from Bordeaux, nothing is better than a dry white wine to cure kidney stones. To endorse the point, he engaged in frequent cures using this precious diuretic liquid.

It is said that the Dutch philosopher, Erasmus, put an end to his stomach pains by drinking wine from the region of Burgundy.

Ambroise Paré, doctor and surgeon to the royal family of France, healed the wounds of his patients using bandages soaked in red wine.

What is also interesting, is that specific wines were seen to have specific effects. For instance, when Louis XIV was suffering with gout, his doctor used to replace his bottle of Burgundy with a bottle of Champagne.

PHYSIOLOGICAL EFFECTS AND PROPERTIES OF WINE

The nutritional and therapeutic properties of wine are now recognised by modern science. It goes without saying that the results are dependent on the quality of the wine and that consumption in large quantities is not advised.

Wine is a food

Wine has nutritional value and contains essential elements that the body is readily able to assimilate.

Wine is a tonic

The tonic effect of wine comes principally from tannin. The more tannin it contains, the greater are its invigorating effects, both physical and psychological.

Wine is thus a natural means of recuperating after heavy physical exertion.

Red wine, especially if it is old, is recommended during periods of convalescence, for fighting infectious diseases and serious viruses.

Wine is an antidepressant

Professor Fiessinger claimed that "wine maintains a perfect balance between the views of the mind and the play of emotions."

Wine helps cure depression in that it provokes a certain feeling of euphoria. It is recommended, in particular, to patients who must follow a restrictive diet for therapeutic reasons. Without doubt, a fine vintage is less toxic than any synthetic product sold at your local chemist's shop.

Wine helps digestion

In the words of Paul and Saint Benedict, a quality wine, in moderate amounts, enjoyed during a meal, facilitates the process of digestion. Wine is rich in vitamin B,[3] which regenerates the liver and assists in the elimination of toxins. These vitamins play an important role in the metabolism of proteins and carbohydrates.

Furthermore, wine also stimulates secretion of gastric juices and facilitates the digestion of proteins (meats and fish). Red wine, rich in tannin, acts on the intestinal muscle fibres, improving the peristaltic action and relieving constipation. A fine vintage is usually an efficient means to treat spasmodic colitis (inflammation of the colon).

According to Doctor Maury, Cardinal Richelieu – an influential advisor to the French king, Louis XIII – suffered from "intestinal languor". He cured himself by regularly drinking a Bordeaux wine, now known as "the Richelieu infusion".

Wine is a diuretic

Wine and particularly white wine, is a diuretic. Hippocrates had already discovered this and recommended it to his patients. We have already seen how Montaigne scrupulously drank white wine to cleanse his kidneys. Acidic white wines (Chardonnay, Pinot Blanc, Zinfandel, Amador and Champagnes) are rich in tartrate and potassium sulphates. These elements, which promote the proper elimination of toxins, are good for the kidneys.

Wine replenishes body minerals

Wine contains a high concentration of minerals that are easily assimilated by the body, including calcium, potassium, magnesium, silicon, zinc,

---

[3] As we have seen in the preceding chapter, sugar and other carbohydrates can lead to a vitamin B deficiency.

fluoride, copper, manganese, chrome and sulphuric mineral anion.

Wine as a bactericide

There have been indications since ancient times, that wine was a bactericide. This has verified on many occasions and in particular during epidemics. In 1886, Rambuteau noted that wine drinkers were less prone to cholera than water drinkers. In 1892, polluted water was not considered dangerous if it was mixed with one third the quantity of wine. A few years later, doctors began to prescribe wine to help cure typhoid fever. More recently, Professor Masquelier, of the University of Bordeaux, demonstrated the bactericidal effects of red Bordeaux on colibacillosis, polluted water and vegetables. At the same time, two Canadian researchers discovered that red wine attacked certain viruses, particularly polio and herpes.[4]

Finally, it is important to note that the antiseptic properties of wine are in proportion to its age. A young wine that is drunk soon after fermentation (such as a Beaujolais Nouveau) is not a very effective bactericide.

Wine fights allergies

In the 19th century, those with sensitive skin were advised to dip their strawberries in wine to avoid skin rashes.

Professor Masquelier demonstrated that wine worked as an anti-histamine and, thus, prevented allergies. He also noted that the rich manganese and vitamin P content in certain wines, like Côtes de Ventoux, Corbieres and Minervois, had the same effect.

Wine has a beneficial effect on the cardiovascular system

It is here that wine has been shown to have the greatest benefit.

As early as 1786, the British doctor Heberden discovered that wine relieved the pain associated with angina. More recently, Professor Masquelier found that the elements contained in wine were capable of preventing myocardial infarct.

[4] Herpes: a viral disease characterised by the formation of blisters on the skin or on mucous membranes.

In 1979, an exhaustive study conducted in Britain revealed that among 18 Western countries, the number of deaths due to heart attack was lowest amongst those populations that habitually consumed wine.

It was therefore concluded that wine worked as a protective agent against arteriosclerosis.

In 1982, after years of research, Professor Masquelier, discovered which elements in wine were responsible for this protective action.

According to Masquelier, the procyanidines in wine are able to control at least three factors:

1. They accelerate the removal of cholesterol from the blood by opposing the formation of fatty deposits necessary for the build-up of atheroma plaques and reinforcing the effects of vitamin C necessary for eliminating cholesterol.
2. They stabilise the collagen fibres that act as a support for the various arterial membranes.
3. They work against the local production of histamines that are thought to trigger the formation of atheromas.

It is the tannin in the wine which contains the procyanidines, so it is reasonable to conclude that the more tannin there is in the wine, the higher will be the incidence of procyanidines.

Now that the benefits of this substance are being recognised, perhaps the pharmaceutical industry may be tempted to derive from it the miracle cure for cardiovascular disease they have long sought. It would be a wasted effort of course, since the remedy already exists in a much more palatable form than a pharmaceutical preparation.

All of which reminds me of my grandmother, who only drank mature Bordeaux wine and died prematurely at the age of 102.

However, to return to the subject of wine, I would remind you that wine constitutes a dietary lapse as far as Phase One is concerned. It should be introduced into Phase Two, and drunk with moderation according to the following guidelines:

 − never drink wine on an empty stomach;
 − start drinking as late in the meal as possible
 − drink moderately − no more than half a litre a day.

SUGGESTED WINES TO IMPROVE YOUR HEALTH*

Remember, you should take care to drink no more than half a litre a day, bearing in mind that one glass of wine at the end of the meal is enough to benefit from its therapeutic properties.

CLINICAL INDICATION	TREATMENT
Acidosis	Pouilly-Fuisse' – Sancerre *Fume, Blanc, Napa*
Allergies	Corbieres – Medoc – Minervois – Ventoux *Grey Riesling, Monterey – Barbera, Santa Clara – Cabernet, Napa*
Anaemia	Cahors – Cotes-de-nuit – Cotes-de-Beaune – Cotes-de-Graves – Pomerol – Madiran *Pinot Noir; Napa – Pinot Noir, Sonoma – Cabernet, Napa*
Antibiotics (side effects)	Mèdoc – Mercurey *Cabernet, Napa – Pinot Blanc – Senoma*
Arterial lesions	Champagne Brut – Morgon – Saint-Emilion *Cabernet, Senoma*
Arteriosclerosis	Dry champagne – Corsican wines (Ajaccio) Graves – Muscadet – wines from Provence – Sancerre – Saint-Emilion *Champagne, Napa, Sonoma, Mendocino – Zinfandel, Amador – French Colombard, Mendocino – Fumé Blanc, Napa – Cabernet, Sonoma*
Arthritis	Asace – Chablis – Crépy – Minervois – Pouilly – Saint-Veran – Seyssel *Gewurztraminer Sonoma – Muscat of Alexandria – Pinot Blanc, Monterey – Emerald Riesling, Santa Clara – Johannisberg Riesling, Monterey – Sylvaner, Monterey – Pinot Noir Rosé, Sonoma*
Arthrosis	Rosé wines from Provence (Bandol – Cassis)
Asthma	Corbières – Minervois *Grey Riesling, Monterey – Barbera, Santa Clara*
Bile insufficiency	Anjou – Vouvray *California Grenache Rosé – Chenin Blanc, Napa – California Chenin Blanc*
Bloating	Dry Champagne – Gaillac-perlé *Champagne, Napa, Sonoma, Mendocino – California Sparkling Muscat*

* This table is from Dr. Maury's book "Wine is the Best Medecine".

CLINICAL INDICATION	TREATMENT
Breast feeding	Graves reds – Beaujolais – Blanquette de Limoux *Zinfandel, Amador – California Zinfandel- California Gamay Beaujolais Nouveau*
Bronchitis	Julienas – Médoc – Moulin-à-vent – Muscat de Rivesaltes *Cabernet, Napa – Gamay, Beaujolais, Monterey*
Calcium deficiency	Arbois – Champigny – Corbières – Côtes-de-Beaune – Côtes-de-Nuit – Côtes-du-Rhone – Madiran – Maury – Premiers Côtes-de-Bordeaux – Saint-Emilion – Saumurois *Grey Riesling, Monterey – Barbera, Santa Clara – Pinot Noir, Napa – Pinot Noir, Sonoma – California Zinfandel – Cabernet, Sonoma*
Cholelithiasis	Touraine dry white wines
Cholesterol	Alsace – Muscadet – Provence rosé *Gewurztraminer, Sonoma – Muscat of Alexandria – Pinot Blanc, Monterey – Emerald Riesling, Monterey – Sylvaner, Monterey – Pinot Noir Rosé, Sonoma*
Colibacillosis	Champagne brut – Médoc *Cabernet, Napa*
Colitis (and gastroenteritis)	White Gaillac – Gaillac perlé
Constipation	White Anjou – Bandol – White Bergerac – Cassis – Jurançon – Montravel doux – Morgon – Pécharmant *Chenin Blanc, Napa – California Chenin Blanc*
Convalescence	Médoc – Corsican wines – Frontignan – Red Graves – Mercurey – Monbazillac – Vouvray *Cabernet, Napa – Zinfandel, Amador – Pinot Blanc, Sonoma – Chenin Blanc Napa – California Chenin Blanc*
Cystitis	White Anjous
Depression	Chablis – Médoc-Listrac *Chardonnay, Sonoma – Chardonnay, Napa – Pinot Blanc, Napa – Pinot Blanc, Sonoma – Cabernet, Napa*
Diabetes	Champagne brut – White Gaillac – Muscadet – wines of Provence – Sancerre *Fumé Blanc Napa*
Diarrhoea	Beaujolais – Madiran – Médoc *California Zinfandel, California Gamay Superior – Gamay, Napa – Gamay Beaujolais, Monterey*

CLINICAL INDICATION	TREATMENT
Dyspepsia	White Anjou – Champagne brut – Iroulegy – Monbazillac – Montlouis – Vouvray *Champagne, Napa, Sonoma, Mendocino – Chenin Blanc, Napa – California Chenin Blanc*
Eczema	Sylvaner – Gros-Plant – Muscadet – Dry Jurançon *Sylvaner, Monterey – French Colombard, Mendocino*
Emaciation	Musca-du-Cap-Corse – Muscat-Banyuls
Fatigue (see stimulants)	Médoc – Pouilly-Fuissé – Puligny-Montrachet *Cabernet, Napa – Chardonnay, Napa*
Fever	Champagne – Julienas – Médoc – Moulin-à-Vent *Champagne, Napa, Sonoma, Mendocino – California Sparkling Muscat*
Flu	Champagne brut – Côtes-Rotie – Morgon – Saint-Emilion *Champagne, Napa, Sonoma, Mendocino – California Petite Sirah – Cabernet, Sonoma*
Gallstones	Anjou – Vouvray *California Grenache Rosé – Chenin Blanc, Napa – California Chenin Blanc*
Gout	Province rosé – White Savoie – Sancerre – Champagne *Fumé Blanc, Napa*
Haemorrhages (tendency to)	Côtes-de-Beaune Cahors l'écharmant Saint-Emilion *Pinot Noir, Sonoma – Cabernet, Sonoma*
Hyperchlorydria	Sauternes – Barsac *Johannisberg Riesling (white), Monterey*
Hypertension (High blood pressure)	Alsace – Chablis – White graves – Pouilly-Fuissé – Sancerre *Gewurztraminer, Sonoma – Muscat of Alexandria – Pinot Blanc, Monterey – Emerald Riesling, Santa Clara – Johannisberg Riesling, Monterey – Sylvaner, Monterey – Pinot Noir Rosé, Sonoma – Chardonnay, Sonoma – Chardonnay, Napa – Pinot Blanc, Napa – Pinot Blanc, Sonoma – Zinfandel, Amador (white) – Fumé Blanc, Napa*
Hypoglycaemia	Muscat-de-Banyuls – Muscat-de-Corse – Muscat-de-Frontignan

133

CLINICAL INDICATION	TREATMENT
Hypotension (Low blood pressure)	Côtes-de-Beaune (red) – Beaujolais – Château-Chalon – Roussillon wines *Pinot Noir, Sonoma – California Zinfandel – California Gamay Beaujolais Nouveau – Gamay, Napa – Gamay Beaujolais – Chilled California Dry Sherry*
Infarcts (tendency to)	Dry champagne – Blanc de blanc – aged Bordeaux *Champagne, Napa, Sonoma, Mendocino*
Kidney stones	Pouilly-Fuissé – Sancerre – Seyssel
Lithaemia	Gros-Plan – Muscadet – White Saumur – Savoie wines – Sylvaner *California Champagne – French Colombard, Mendocino – Sylvaner, Monterey*
Loss of appetite	Banyuls – Jurançon – Frontignan – Monbazillac – Sauternes *Johannisberg Riesling (white), Monterey*
Low-sodium diet	Chablis – Dry champagne *Chardonnay, Sonoma – Chardonnay, Napa – Pinot Blanc, Napa – Pinot Blanc, Sonoma*
Menopause	Red Burgundy – Cahors – Saint-Emilion – Pécharmant *Pinot Noir, Napa – Pinot Noir, Sonoma – Cabernet, Sonoma*
Mineral deficiencies	Premiers Côtes-de-Bordeaux – Châteauneuf-du-Pape – Gevrey-Chambertin – Clos-Vougeot *Petite Sirah, Napa and Sonoma – California Sauvignon Blanc*
Muscular spasms	Red Côtes-de-Provence – Red Côtes-du-Rhone *California Zinfandel (red)*
Neurosis	Blanquette-de-Limoux – Red Irougely
Obesity	Alsace – White Bergerac – White Gaillac – Dry Montravel – Pouilly *Gewurztraminer, Sonoma – Muscat of Alexandria – Pinot Blanc, Monterey – Emerald Riesling, Santa Clara – Johannisberg Riesling, Monterey – Sylvaner, Monterey – Pinot Noir Rosé, Sonoma*
Oedema	Chablis – Crépy – Muscadet – Sylvaner *Chardonnay, Sonoma – Chardonnay, Napa – Pinot Blanc, Napa – Pinot Blanc, Sonoma – French Colombard, Mendocino – Sylvaner, Monterey*
Osteoporosis	Côtes-de-Nuit – Côtes-du-Rhone – Médoc *Pinot Noir, Napa – California Zinfandel – Cabernet, Sonoma*

CLINICAL INDICATION	TREATMENT
Phosphorus deficiency	Dry or semi-dry champagne – Clairette-de-Die *Champagne, Napa, Sonoma, Mendocino*
Resistance to polio (prevention of)	Médoc – Mercurey *Cabernet, Napa – Pinot Blanc, Sonoma*
Resistance to viral and infectious diseases	Red Bordeaux – Red Burgundy – Côtes-du-Ventoux *Ruby Cabernet, Santa Clara – California French Colombard –* *Zinfandel, Amador – Cabernet, Napa – Merlot, Napa –* *Cabernet, Sonoma – Pinot Noir, Napa – Pinot Noir, Sonoma*
Rheumatism (chronic)	Dry champagne – Corbières – White Gaillac – Minervois *Champagne, Napa, Sonoma, Mendocino*
Rickets	Saint-Emilion *Cabernet, Sonoma*
Senescence (old age)	Aloxe-Corton – Natural champagne *Champagne, Napa, Sonoma, Mendocino*
Sore throat	Médoc – Julienas – Moulin-à-vent *Cabernet, Napa – Gamay, Beaujolais, Monterey*
Sports (diets for)	Chablis – Côtes-de-Nuit *Chardonnay, Sonoma – Chardonnay, Napa – Pinot Blanc,* *Napa – Pinot Blanc, Sonoma*
Stimulants	Champagne brut – Pouilly-Fuissé – Médoc *Champagne, Napa, Sonoma, Mendocino – Cabernet, Napa*
Stomach prolapse	Dry Champagne or Brut *Champagne, Napa, Sonoma, Mendocino – California Spark-* *ling Muscat*
Stomach (sluggishness)	Médoc *Cabernet, Napa*
Suppurations	Bourgueil – Chinon – Corsican wines – Lirac – Premiers Côtes-de-Bordeaux – Tavel – Madiran *California Zinfandel – California Grenache*
Tonics	Côtes-de-Nuit – Côtes-de-Beaune – Cahors – Corbières – Jurançon – Iroulegy – Roussillon wines
Tuberculosis	Champagne dry or brut – Médoc – Mercurey *Champagne, Napa, Sonoma, Mendocino – California Spark-* *ling Muscat*
Ulcers (skin)	Red Bordeaux – Red Burgundy *Ruby Cabernet, Santa Clara – California French Colombard –* *Zinfandel, Amador – Cabernet, Napa – Merlot, Napa –* *Cabernet, Sonoma – Pinot Noir, Napa – Pinot Noir, Sonoma*

CLINICAL INDICATION	TREATMENT
Urine retention	Chablis – Gros-Plan – Muscadet – Pouilly-Fuissé – Sancerre – Savoie wines *Chardonnay, Sonoma – Chardonnay, Napa – Pinot Blanc, Napa – Pinot Blanc, Sonoma*
Urticaria	Corbières – Côtes-de-Ventoux – Médoc – Minervois *Cabernet, Napa*
Vegetarian (diet)	Médoc – Red Beaujolais *Cabernet, Napa – California Zinfandel – California Gamay Beaujolais Nouveau – Gamay, Napa – Gamay Beaujolais, Monterey*
Vitamin deficiency	All red wines
Weight loss	Beaune red – Corsican wines *Pinot Noir, Sonoma*

Beneath the French wines, suggested American counterparts in italics.
The information contained in the list above, should not be interpreted or substituted for an actual medical prescription. Consult your doctor if in doubt.

5

The Genius of Chocolate

Christopher Columbus discovered chocolate in the Caribbean during his fourth voyage in search of the Indies in 1502.

The strange drink was first offered to him by the Aztec chief of an island where he made a short stop. Columbus and his crew found the brew quite repulsive, and never tried it again. Perhaps this is not surprising, as we are told that the local recipe was rather bitter and spicy.

It was not until Cortes discovered Mexico in 1519, that the Europeans came to recognise its real worth – rather more for its economic value than for its taste.

Cocoa beans constituted the wealth of Mexico and were the only means of trade and barter in the land. The Spaniards therefore needed to obtain the beans in order to gain access to the local riches, particularly the gold. Moreover, since wine was not available, the Spanish soldiers eventually took to this "chocolat" and noticed that "when you drink it, you can travel all day without being tired and without needing food".

They soon discovered they could lessen the bitterness with sugar, and add vanilla, cinnamon or aniseed to the cocoa. Thanks to the priestesses of Oaxaca[1] who came up with the first recipes, chocolate at last became delicious.

From that moment, the European colonists came to understand the financial possibilities of this new discovery. So they decided to settle in this "New World" in the hope of making their fortunes.

Chocolate quickly became part of Spanish life. Unable to give up this exotic product when they returned to Spain, the colonists soon assured its popularity among their fellow countrymen. The import market grew and from then on, the chocolate trade routes were established.

---

[1] A town in Southern Mexico at the foot of the Sierra Madre mountains, found in 1486 by the Aztecs and occupied by the Spaniards until 1522.

However, it took many years for chocolate to cross the frontiers of Spain. It was not until the 17th century that it began to appear throughout the rest of Europe.

In France, chocolate made its debut in the court of Louis XIII in 1615 when the king married Anne of Austria, daughter of Philip II of Spain. The child queen loved chocolate and introduced her "passion" to the rest of France. The Cardinal of Lyon, brother of Richelieu, often drank chocolate "to calm his spleen and appease his rage and foul temper." As for Cardinal Mazarin[2], he would never travel without his personal Italian chocolate-maker. At his levee each morning, the Regent Philip of Orleans would organise what you might have called a "chocolate party" had he not been the only person drinking the stuff. To be admitted to "The Regent's Chocolate" however, was considered a great privilege.

The virtues of chocolate

Without doubt, more has been written about chocolate than any other food. For who can remain indifferent to chocolate?

Besides its delicious taste, commentators during the 17th and 18th centuries make great play of its therapeutic properties. At first it was prescribed to "reconstitute the natural forces in the body", though today we can attribute its invigorating effects to a high concentration of magnesium. Also rich in phosphorus, chocolate was recommended to "scholars" to help sustain them in their intellectual endeavours.

Ecclesiastics found that chocolate helped them endure the fasts to which they were regularly subjected, particularly Lent.

The majority of commentators agreed in recognising the digestive virtues of chocolate. Brillat-Savarin, father of all food critics, observes in his "Physiology of Taste" that "if you take an ample cup of chocolate after having eaten a copious lunch, within three hours your digestion will be complete". He also claims that he persuaded several ladies to try the experience for themselves and that they never failed to be amazed and lost in admiration for him.

In her remarkable book on chocolate, Martine Jolly[3] quotes a certain Doctor Blegny, who recommends a chocolate prepared by himself to

---

[2] H succeeded Richelieu and was also a personal advisor to the king.
[3] Martine Jolly, "*The Devouring Passion of Chocolate*".

"those who love and are unfortunate enough to suffer the most universal of all gallant illnesses, for they will find (in chocolate) the most enlightening consolation".

Other 18th century contemporaries of Blegny claimed that chocolate cured tuberculosis.

These then are the virtues of chocolate. If you love it, you will no doubt find others to add to the list.

If you love chocolate you may indulge but not abuse it. If I were to claim you could eat it at every meal, you would find my method somewhat contradictory. Because however delicious it may be, chocolate is still a carbohydrate-lipid.

Fortunately its fats are of the type which will help lower your cholesterol level. So, for it to be only a slight imbalance in your diet, it should do two things: contain as little carbohydrate as possible and consist of as much "good" fat as possible. In other words, a "good" lipid with a low carbohydrate content, is in every way compatible with our method.

So the first thing we must do, is select a high-quality chocolate with at least 60% cocoa. The percentage of cocoa is always written on the wrapping. Chocolate with around 70% cocoa is fairly easy to obtain and is a far better alternative. For those who want the best, I have produced a chocolate with 85% cocoa, which you can get from the Montignac Boutique in London. In my view, not only does a high cocoa content reduce the percentage of carbohydrates, it also tastes much better.

The second strategy is to choose chocolate desserts with no flour or sugar (or the absolute minimum). The chocolate mousse and the bitter chocolate cake (the recipes are in the appendix) are perfect examples. For the past ten years, these two recipes have been my specialities, and I can assure you that my family and friends are mad about them.

I must emphasise again however, that chocolate remains a discrepancy, and should be treated as such. It is not allowed in Phase One. During Phase Two, it can be enjoyed bearing in mind the reservations I have just expressed.

One of the best moments in the day to indulge in chocolate is in the middle of the afternoon on an empty stomach. Two or three squares of dark bitter chocolate containing a minimum of 70% cocoa, will create only a slight dietary imbalance as far as our method is concerned. So spoil yourself.

Chocolate is an anti-depressant[4], so elect to eat it when you are feeling low, to raise your spirits or just for the pleasure of it.

One last piece of advice to conclude this chapter.

I suggest that if you find yourself becoming a chocolate fancier, be careful not to let your passion degenerate into an addiction.

Should you find you find that one piece of chocolate is beginning to lead to another and you have difficulty in controlling yourself, a worth-while tip is to take a good drink of cold water.

[4] Se "*Les vertus thérapeutiques du chocolat*" Dr.H. Robert – Ed Artulen.

6

Sport Does not Cause Weight Loss

In his song, "Tu t'laisses aller" ("You're letting yourself go"), the French singer Charles Aznavour advises his girlfied who is a bit of a lump, to "Indulge in a little sport to lose some weight!"

Here we have a widely accepted view which goes by default. It is quite clear that Aznavour never had a weight problem, or he would have realised that, contrary to popular belief, *sport has never caused anyone to lose weight.*

When you became concerned with your excess weight, I suppose, like everyone else, you decided to take up some form of sport – either jogging or cycling, or sometimes both at once.

Having tried both, I can assure you the results are a complete let-down!

Exercise is wonderful to unwind, to let off steam, to invigorate oneself, to get together with friends or to get out of the house. But, do not think it is the answer to losing weight if you continue to eat as unhealthily as most people do.

Exercising to lose weight goes hand in hand with the caloric myth. When you take up a sport with the intention of shedding weight, you will have a tendency to measure the success of your efforts by the amount you perspire.

What you are actually losing, is water. Do not think you are "burning calories," because you are only expending energy from your temporary reserves of glycogen, which are replaced by your consumption of carbo-hydrates.

The first time you go back to doing some sport, you may indeed notice the loss of the odd hundred grams if your scales are sufficiently reliable and accurate.

However, if you have got into the habit of exercising regularly – every

Saturday for example – your body will gradually readjust its supply of energy to meet your new demands. As these increase, your body will quickly start storing enough glycogen to cope.

You will very rapidly notice that not only are you not losing any weight, you may in fact be back where you started from. It is even possible you may even have gained some weight.

Remember the hungry dog that buries its bone? If your physical exertion increases, not only will your body produce more energy, but, being cautious, it will also stock up its fat reserves. And so the vicious circle begins.

You decide to add 3 miles to your cycling route to outwit your body. However, programmed to understand the laws of the market, your computer will make adjustments.

This is how, for a few grams less, not only do you gain a few grams more but you run some serious health risks. For in sport there is one rule you must never forget: "never push your body beyond its limits." You would never drive from John O'Groats to Land's End in a dilapidated old banger. Similarly, do not set goals for yourself that are too ambitious for your age, your physical condition or your level of training.

Engage in sport for all the traditional reasons or just for pleasure, but do not expect it to solve your weight problem by doing it unless you change your eating habits as well.

Adopting the eating method presented in this book when you take up exercise, will enable you to accelerate the weight-loss process in Phase One. But more importantly, your physical efforts will contribute to re-establishing the natural metabolic rhythm of your body, by suppressing insulin-resistance and hyperinsulinism more quickly.

In Phase One, your glycogen is mainly made up by the breaking-down of your fat reserves. If you increase demand, your fat mass should disappear more rapidly.

Physical exertion is particularly beneficial for the obese whose fat cells do not respond properly to insulin (insulin resistance), thus leading the pancreas to produce a surplus (hyperinsulinism).

Moreover, obesity upsets thermogenesis – the production of heat. So, paradoxically, the fatter the individual, the lower the energy expended on physical effort.

The alimentary principles of this method and a reasonable amount of physical exertion are entirely compatible and will contribute to a successful return to normal weight.

7

A Practice Run in One of the Best Restaurants in Paris

When one of my friends or colleagues comes to me with the serious intent of finding a solution to his weight problem, I usually suggest a practice run.

We go to a restaurant and I begin my explanations. The theory is important, but you will agree that in these matters, practice is indispensable.

This is why, when I decided to write this book, one of my first ideas was to write a chapter in which I would demonstrate in a concrete way, how my method could be applied in one of the restaurants where I used to eat.

For practical reasons, I first thought that the idea could be based on the menus of a dozen restaurants situated in Paris. But I soon realised this would be very boring for my reader, given the similar nature of most menus.

Furthermore, I was in a quandary over which restaurants to select. So I decided to choose just one. But then, which one? What would I base my choice on? Three stars in the Michelin Guide? The "Super four chefs hats" in the Gault-Millau guide? Or the one closest to my home or my office?

As luck would have it, the decision turned out to be easier than anticipated.

One Sunday afternoon on the Bordeaux-Paris train, I was rereading one of the first chapters of my manuscript, when at Saint-Pierre-des-Corps, I was joined in my compartment by a man who looked vaguely familiar, despite the absence of his famous chef's hat. It was Joël Robuchon.[1]

So, with his permission we will now carefully dissect his menu for the month of February 1986, applying the method that I hope you are about to try.

---

[1] Owner of "Jamin", one of the most famous restaurants in France at the time.

MENU

Saucisson au foie gras*
Duck sausage with foie gras

Frivolité de saumon fumé au caviar
Smoked salmon and caviar

Lapereau mitonné en gelée aux legumes
Simmered baby rabbit in a vegetable aspic

Gelée de caviar à la creme de choux-fleur
Caviar gelée with a cauliflower purée

Salade de homard breton au Bolero
Breton lobster salad "au Bolero"

Ravioli de langoustine aux choux**
Prawn ravioli with cabbage

Foie gras chaud à la creme de lentilles**
Warm foie gras with cream of lentils

Galette de truffes aux oignons et lard fumé
Truffle crêpes with onions and smoked bacon

Fricassé de langoustines aux champignons de courgettes
Prawn fricassé with mushrooms and courgettes

Medley d'huitres et de noix de Saint-Jacques au caviar*
Oysters and scallops with caviar

Rouelles de homard à la vapeur aux herbes en civet
Steamed lobster with stewed herbs

Soupe crèmeuse au potiron
Cream of pumpkin soup

Entree (Fish)

Merlan aux épices et aux encornets
Spiced whitefish and squid

Etuvée de homard et de noix de Saint-Jacques aux truffes**
Baked lobster and scallops with truffles – Served with fresh pasta

Blanc de bar cuit en peau, sauce verjutée
White bass served with a verjuice sauce

Homard meunière aux fins aromates
Longtailed lobster with aromatic herbs

Entree (Meats)

Ris de veau truffé aux asperges
Truffled calf sweetbreads with asparagus

Agneau pastoral aux herbes en salade
Pastoral lamb with herb salad

La fameuse fête de cochon mijotée "IIe de France"
The famous stewed pig's head "IIe de France"

Volaille truffée en Vessie, sauce fleurette
Truffled turkey in a cream sauce – Served with fresh pasta –

Rôti d'agneau aux herbes, en croûte de sel**
Roast lamb with herbs in a salt crust

Mignonnettes de chevreuil poêlées à l'Aigre doux*
Filet of young goat stir-fried in a sweet and sour sauce

Cheese-board

Desserts

Chaud-froid de pommes à la pistache ou à la canelle*
Hot and cold apple pie with pistachio or cinnamon

Crême caramelisée à la cassonade*
Creme caramel with brown sugar

Gratin de Fruits * Clafoutis de poires au miel**
Pears baked in batter with honey

Soupe de fruits au vin rouge*
Fruit soup with red wine

Mousse au chocolat*
Chocolate mousse

Tarte à l'orange**
Orange tart

Tarte au citron**
Lemon tart

Sorbets*
Nougat glacé au coulis de framboise
Frozen nougat draped in raspberry sauce ***

* Dishes containing carbohydrates, but in small quantities
** Dishes containing carbohydrates, enough to create an imbalance.
In **Phase One** avoid all dishes with asterisks.
In **Phase Two** avoid all dishes with two asterisks.

147

We will study the menu in the same way as we approached our method. We will look at both parts: weight loss (Phase One) and weight maintenance (Phase Two).

If you are in Phase One

Here is what you should select:

- *Aperitif:* Tomato juice or sparkling water with a slice of lemon.
- *Starter:* You may opt for any of the starters except those that contain even the smallest amount of carbohydrate.

You should avoid:

- "Saucisson de canard au foie gras"*
  Duck sausage with foie gras,
- "Ravioli de langoustines aux choux"**
  Prawn ravioli with cabbage,
- "Foie gras chaud à la crème de lentilles,"**
  Warm foie gras with cream of lentils,
- "Medley d'huitres et de noix de Saint-Jacques au caviar"*
  Oysters and scallops with caviar.

- *Main Dish:* Again, you can pick any dish except those that contain carbohydrates, or are served with carbohydrates.

In Phase I, you should avoid choosing:

- "Etuvée de homard et de noix de Saint-Jacques aux truffes"**
  Baked lobster and scallops with truffles,
- "Le rôti d'agneau aux herbes en croûte de sel"**
  Roast lamb with herbs in a salty crust,
- "Mignonnette de chevreuil pôlée à l'aigre doux"*
  Filet of young goat stir-fried in sweet and sour sauce.

These three dishes should be avoided because the first two are accompanied by fresh pasta and the third is served with a quince and bilberry sauce.

- *Dessert:* Cheese only.
- *Drink:* Water or a small glass of wine that can be enjoyed with the cheese at the end of the meal.

If you are in Phase Two

As you have learned, in this phase you can order anything as long as you intelligently administer a proper balance.

First, try to identify what would upset your balance – in other words, anything that contains carbohydrates.

The following items are included in this category:

- "Foie gras chaud a la crème de lentilles"**
  Warm foie gras with cream of lentils (because of the lentils),
- "Ravioli aux langoustines aux choux"**
  Prawn ravioli with cabbage,
- the two dishes served with fresh pasta (the baked lobster and the roast lamb),**
- desserts**

If you wish to order a dessert – which is what I would recommend since they are excellent – avoid, in your choice of entree, the two dishes served with fresh pasta. If, on the other hand, you decide you cannot resist the fresh pasta, avoid one of the starters we have already mentioned, and if you really want a dessert, choose a sorbet*, a "gratin de fruit"* or a "creme caramel"* which contain only have small quantities of carbohydrates.

As always, avoid the bread (home-made at Robuchon's), but you may drink whatever you wish (always in reasonable amounts), starting with a glass of champagne as an aperitif.

Conclusion

I hope that in reading this book you have found the answers to your questions. In any case, I hope you have enjoyed it.

I, for one, took great pleasure in writing it, because the research I did, enabled me to organise in my mind information that I had accumulated haphazardly over the years.

In my researches and in putting the book together, I have become more and more convinced that "We are what we eat!"

In other words, our present physical condition is the result of what we have consumed in the past. And since I am speaking to an audience of "managers" I can say freely what I am sure you have already understood – namely, that your energy, dynamism, competitiveness, ambition and strength all depend on your diet.

If you learn to manage what you eat, you will learn to manage your life.

Unfortunately, modern man is no longer a very sensible being. He has lost most of his wisdom. Today he is able to walk on the moon but does not know how to manage his diet.

Zoo-keepers take great interest in studying animals' eating habits. They know that therein lies the key to survival.

When the female monkey is no longer fertile, when a bear's hide has lost its fur, when the lion becomes docile or when the elephant loses its memory, the zoo-keeper checks it out and adjusts the animal's diet accordingly.

When, at the dawn of the twenty-first century, the average man wakes up with a frightening rash on his face, a splitting headache or foul breath, it is highly probable that his doctor will not even ask about his diet. Animals and machines often get better attention than humans.

150

Conclusion

Governments of industrialised countries should be more concerned with the inadequate way their citizens feed themselves and give priority to this atrocious problem. Were they to pursue an informed, vigorous and extended campaign to educate the public in this fundamental area of public health, the dividends in increased productivity, reduced costs to the national health services and improved quality of life for many more of its citizens – both rich and poor – would be enormous.

Some time ago I visited Disney World in Florida and, as I stood among a typical American crowd, I was truly scandalised at the obesity I saw. Approximately 18% of all Americans are obese. That is almost one in five of the people you meet. It is a situation which experts in America acknowledge is due to collective intoxication by "bad" carbohydrates.

With this number of obese people, it is not surprising that obesity has been accepted as part of the everyday life of the United States. Fashion lines are created especially for the bulky woman and business suits are available up to the size "Extra-Extra Large".

The most distressing aspect of all, is that the greatest percentage of obese people are among today's youth – which seems to prove that the phenomenon is directly linked to eating habits developed since the Second World War.

In France, I believe we may be able to resist this trend because of our culinary traditions. However, the American experience is no longer at the embryonic stage in France. Hamburger bars are appearing in all our major cities and the consumption of soft drinks is booming.

By yielding to publicity and practicality, we are involuntarily encouraging our children to develop eating habits we would not necessarily accept ourselves. In a few years, it may be too late to do anything.

Many people could explain to you in detail how to make a car last for 100,000 miles, but they have no idea how to prolong the lives of their children. Tragically, it seems not to be of widespread concern.

The human body is a remarkable "machine", capable of enduring so much that it not easy to detect when it has reached "the danger zone".

Women are generally at less risk than men, since they are endowed with greater physical sensitivity. They are therefore more able (indeed,

151

they are compelled) to behave sensibly and take greater care of their bodies.

A man, because of his "virility", by nature does not know his limits. He will carry on pushing himself until eventually something gives. You are probably aware of some of the signs.

Your body has recorded all the nutritional mistakes you have made since childhood, and has undertaken a number of procedures to handle them. You will probably have felt the side effects of these reactions (headaches, stomach pains, digestive troubles, liver problems). They are the signs that your body is reaching its limit: your body is showing signs of weakness by becoming more sensitive.

The symptoms vary from one individual to another, but the underlying reason is generally the same – an unhealthy diet.

Consider yourself lucky, because, by looking for a means of losing weight, you have now found the solution to a number of other ailments from which you have been suffering – particularly a lack of vitality.

This is exactly what happened to me a few of years ago.

When I was in college, I was studying at an institute that prepared students for senior administrative jobs in industry, public life and politics, although I chose a completely different course.

On the first day of term, the Director gathered the students together and concluded his address with the following words, which I have never forgotten:

"As Director of this establishment whilst you are here, my only goal will be to teach you to read, to write and to speak."

As the author of this book, my only goal has been to teach you how to eat.

Table 1

List of Permitted Foods
Phase One: Weight Loss

STARTERS	CARBO-HYDRATE FOODS	MAIN COURSE	VEGETABLES/ SALADS	DESSERTS
Eggs	Beans	Meat	Tomatoes	Yoghurt
Unsmoked	Lentils	(except liver)	Spinach	Cheese
Ham	Wholewheat	Cooked Meats	Chicory	Desserts based
Salads	Pasta	Fish (all)	Lettuce	on Egg
Tomato	Brown Rice	Poultry	Cress	Custards
–French	(All without	Rabbit	Lamb's	
Beans	oils, fats)	Lobster	Lettuce	
–Chicory		Eggs	Dandelion	
–Cucumber			Aubergines	
–Cauliflower		*Dressings*	Celery	
Radishes			Cabbage	
Leeks		Butter	Cauliflower	
Lettuce, etc.		Olive Oil	Sauerkraut	
Celery		Peanut Oil	French Beans	
Mushrooms		Margarine	Turnips	
Asparagus		Mayonnaise	Leeks	
Smoked		Béarnaise	Peppers	
Salmon		Sauce	Courgettes	
Tuna		Salt, Pepper	Broccoli	
Fresh		Onions,	Fennel	
Salmon		Garlic	Sorrel	
Sardines		Shallots	Mushrooms	
Mussels		Herbs	etc.	
Crab				
Lobster				

NB This chart does not list all the permitted foods, just a
selection of some common ones

Table 2

List of Permitted Foods
Phase Two: Maintaining a Stable Weight

STARTERS	CARBO-HYDRATE FOODS	MAIN COURSE	VEGETABLES/SALADS	DESSERTS
Foie Gras*	Beans	Meat (all)	Tomatoes	Raspberries*
Eggs	Lentils	Cooked Meats	Spinach	Strawberries*
Cooked	Wholewheat	Fish (all)	Chicory	Melon
Meats	Pasta	Poultry	Lettuce	Yogurt
Salads:	Brown Rice	Rabbit	Cress	Fromage Frais
−Tomato	(May be eaten	Lobster	Lamb's	Cheeses
−French	with fats and	Eggs	Lettuce	Coat's
Beans	protein)		Dandelion	Cheeses*
−Chicory		*Dressings*	Aubergine	Cantal
−Walnuts			Celery	Cheese*
−Cucumber		Butter	Cabbage	
−Cauliflower		Olive Oil	Cauliflower	Bavarois*
−Mushrooms		Peanut Oil	Sauerkraut	Charlotte*
Radishes		Margarine	French Beans	Chocolate
Leeks		Mayonnaise	Turnips	Mousse*
Lettuce		Béarnaise	Leeks	Sorbets*
Celery		Sauce	Peppers	Gratin:
Hearts of		Salt	Courgettes	−Raspberry
Palm*		Pepper	Broccoli	−Strawberry
Avocado*		Mustard*	Fennel	−Blackberry
Tuna		Onions	Sorrel	−Redcurrant
Fresh Salmon		Garlic	Mushrooms	
Smoked		Shallots	Salsifi	
Salmon		Herbs	Lentils	
Sardines			Broad Beans	
Mussels			Peas	
Crab			Dried Beans	
Prawns			Chickpeas	
Scampi				
Lobster				
Oysters*				
Scallops*				

NB Foods marked with an asterisk are permitted in moderation.

Chocolate Recipes

Recipe 1

CHOCOLATE MOUSSE

Makes 6 to 8 servings

Ingredients

−14 oz. quality dark chocolate (2 tablets) with at least 60% cocoa
−8 eggs
−3 tbs. rum
−1 orange
−4 tsps. ground coffee
−a pinch of salt

Equipment

−1 electric mixer
−1 large double boiler
−1 grater
−2 large bowls
−1 spatula

Break the chocolate in pieces and put into double boiler. Make half a cup of strong coffee or espresso and add to chocolate with the rum. Melt the chocolate over low heat and smooth mixture with the spatula. If it is too thick, add water.

While the chocolate is melting, grate the orange peel (only use the top part of the skin, the white pith is bitter) and add half to the chocolate mixture. Break the eggs and separate the whites from the yolks. Put in two separate bowls. Beat the egg whites with a pinch of salt until they are very stiff. Lightly whisk the yolks, then add to chocolate mixture. Mix to obtain a smooth and homogenous mixture. Add to whites. Make sure there are no unmixed pieces of chocolate or egg whites at the bottom of the bowl.

Put the mousse in the refrigerator (you can pour it into another bowl if you prefer), but first sprinkle the remaining orange zest on top.

Make the mousse at least five hours prior to serving. Ideally, make it the day before.

Recipe 2

BITTER CHOCOLATE CAKE

Ingredients

−14 oz. quality dark chocolate (2 tablets) with at least 60% cocoa
−10 oz. butter
−2 tbs. cognac
−7 eggs
−1 orange
−4 tsps. ground coffee
−1/4 cup of flour

Equipment

−1 electric mixer
−1 large double boiler
−1 cake mould
−1 grater
−1 spatula
−1 large bowl

Break the chocolate in pieces and put into double boiler. Make half a cup of strong coffee or espresso and add to chocolate with cognac cut the butter in cubes and put it together with the chocolate. Melt chocolate to obtain a smooth and creamy mixture.

Beat the eggs in a bowl while gradually adding the flour. Make sure there are no lumps.

Grate orange peel and add half to chocolate mixture. The orange is optional. If you do not like orange-flavoured chocolate, a superb combination nonetheless, do not add it. If you do, be sure to grate only the top part of the orange since the white pith is bitter. If possible, use a Teflon mould. Be sure it is big enough, as the cake rises 20% during baking. If you do not have an appropriately sized Teflon mould, use aluminium foil greased with butter. Make sure the foil comes up well above the mould.

Add the warm chocolate mixture to the well-beaten eggs and mix until smooth and even. Fill the mould and sprinkle the remaining orange zest on top. Bake at 250° to 350° for 35 minutes.

Let cool at room temperature for 45 minutes before serving.

Cut thin slices (approx. 1/2 inch) that you can serve with two or three tablespoons of custard.

If you make a home-made custard, substitute artificial sweetener for the sugar.

One last piece of advice: if you keep the cake in the refrigerator, take it out at least four hours prior to serving, or the cold may cause it to lose its moistness.

Technical Appendix

Part One

by
Doctor Hervé Robert
Nutritionist

with the collaboration of
Professor Attilio Giacosa,
Head of Nutrition at the
National Cancer Institute (Genoa, Italy)

This document is especially intended for doctors and dietary specialists. Its primary aim is to clarify the concepts of the Montignac Method.

Biography

Doctor Hervé Robert was born in Paris in 1946. A graduate of the Paris School of Medicine (1974), he practised for more than ten years in the rheumatology ward of a local hospital, where he also participated in the operation of a pain-relief centre.

In order to broaden his therapeutic range, he subsequently studied acupuncture, homeopathy, mesotherapy and trace elements. Today he teaches these alternative medical disciplines to his colleagues.

He is the president of the Medical Association of Neuro-Acupuncture and Biostimulation. Acutely aware of the importance of a well-balanced diet in the prevention of certain diseases, he has devoted the last few years to personal research on nutrition.

He is the director of the Institut Vitalité et Nutrition, a non-profitmaking organisation bringing together all French doctors and scientists who practise the Montignac method.

In addition to public conferences and private seminars for various companies, he has helped disseminate the Montignac Method, in collaboration with doctors in the nutrition field from France and other countries.

The former editor of a medical review, he is also the author of a number of articles and several books (Ed. Artulen).

DIETARY BALANCE IN THE MONTIGNAC METHOD DIET

—should be rich in protein;
—should only include 5.25 ounces of meat per day;
—should select poultry rather than meat;
—should include fish (10.5 ounces per week minimum);
—should contain a daily consumption of dairy products (for calcium), preferably non-fat.

FATS

Choose lipids that limit the risks of cardiovascular diseases;
—Limit your consumption of saturated fats (meat, cold cuts, eggs, full fat dairy products);
—Increase your consumption of mono and polyunsaturated vegetable fats (olives, safflower oil);
—Augment your intake of polyunsaturated animal fats (fish).

CARBOHYDRATES

—Elect carbohydrates that prevent hyperglycemic and hyperinsulinic peaks;
—For breakfast, eat breads rich in fiber (whole wheat bread) and cereal;
—Eat fruits;
—Eliminate sugar and refined carbohydrates;
—Use an artificial sweetener if necessary (i.e. Nutrasweet).

FIBER

—Considerably increase the fiber content in your diet: fruits and vegetables (raw or cooked) can be eaten at breakfast and during other meals to provide a healthy daily fiber intake;
—Bring legumes back into your diet.

BEVERAGES

—In the weight-loss phase, it is preferable to drink only water, especially between meals;
—Eliminate chemically sweetened beverages (sodas);

—Avoid distilled alcohols;
—Do not drink too much coffee. Coffee increases the cholesterol levels and stimulates insulin secretion;

FOOD COMPOSITION

Because the Montignac method does not ask you to count calories or weigh your foods, food choices should be made according to their biochemical composition. The foods we eat are made up of the following components:

—proteins
—carbohydrates or sugars
—lipids or fats
—fibers
—water
—mineral salts
—trace elements
—vitamins

In terms of weight-loss, the first four elements are of the most interest to us. However, the others also deserve a few words.

Despite the rich and varied types of food that exist in our countries, we are facing deficiencies in trace elements (selenium, iron, germanium), in mineral salts (magnesium) and in vitamins (folic acid). This is particularly due to the deterioration of the soil.

Although they do not result in major diseases, these minor disequilibria can favor metabolic troubles which explain certain cases of chronic fatigue.

Losing weight means losing fatty mass and not just urinating to eliminate a few pounds of water! Nevertheless, many doctors still prescribe diuretics that only eliminate water. This type of treatment is useless, illusory and even dangerous since it also causes the elimination of useful minerals. In addition, the organism reacts like a sponge, recovering lost water as soon as it can.

It is also important to realize that thyroid extracts rarely affect fatty mass. Instead, they attack the lean muscular mass. They weaken the muscles (causing cramps and fatigue) and can lead to serious troubles in the cardiac muscle. They also disrupt the metabolic function of the thyroid gland. The thyroid is seldom responsible for obesity).

Part One

PROTEINS

A) GENERALITIES

Foods containing nitrogen are called proteins and are vital to nutrition. Proteins are large molecules composed of thousands of amino acids. Amino acids are the building blocks of proteins. There are approximately 20 amino acids required by the human body. Among these, eight must be obtained through food sources since the body is unable to synthesize them independently. These amino acids are isoleucine, leucine, lysine, methionine, phenylalanine, theonine, tryptophane and valine.

These proteins are indispensable to the human body because they:

- build cellular structures,
- are an energy source in the citric acid cycle,
- combine RNA and DNA, which are essential to cellular reproduction,
- synthesize certain hormones and neurotransmitters (e.g. thyroxin and adrenalin),
- blend together bile acids, melanin and respiratory pigments.

Daily protein intake for children and teen-agers should be approximately 60 grams and 90 grams respectively. For adults, the protein intake should represent 15% of the daily energy intake, which is approximately 1 gram per kilo per day. Women should get a minimum of 55 grams and men a minimum of 70 grams.

In 1985, the major sources of protein in the American diet were meat, poultry, and fish (43.4%); dairy products (20.6%); and grain products (19%). On the average, protein intake in the United States is 20–30 percent above the RDA. (Nutrition Monitoring in the United States, pg. 51).

B) PROTEIN SOURCES

1) Animals as a Source of Protein

Proteins are found in meat, cold cuts, poultry, fish, seafood, eggs, milk and dairy products.

The concentration of proteins in 3.5 oz (100 grams) of food is:

*MEAT		*EGGS	
–veal	.70 oz (20.0 g)	–per egg	.45 oz (13.0 g)
–mutton	.56 oz (17.0 g)	*FISH	
–beef	.56 oz (17.0 g)	–tuna	.95 oz (27.0 g)
–pork	.56 oz (17.0 g)	–spotted dogfish	.90 oz (25.0 g)
–lamb	.53 oz (16.0 g)	–mullet	.77 oz (22.0 g)

165

−salami	.90 oz (25.0 g)	−sardines, ray fish, trout	.70 oz (19.0 g)
*COLD CUTS		−mackerel	.65 oz (19.0 g)
−baked ham	.75 oz (20.0 g)	−hake, gilt-head, sole	.60 oz (17.0 g)
−smoked ham	.50 oz (15.0 g)	***SEAFOOD**	
−hot dogs	.50 oz (15.0 g)	−shrimp	.90 oz (25.0 g)
*POULTRY		−crayfish	.80 oz (23.0 g)
−game animals	.77 oz (22.0 g)	−lobster	.55 oz (16.0 g)
−duck	.77 oz (22.0 g)	−squid	.60 oz (17.0 g)
−chicken	.75 oz (21.0 g)	−scallops	.60 oz (17.0 g)
−turkey	.70 oz (20.0 g)	−mussels	.40 oz (11.0 g)
		−oysters	.30 oz (8.0 g)
*DAIRY PRODUCTS			
−cow's milk	.10 oz (3.5 g)	−yogurt	.20 oz (5.2 g)
−sweetened condensed milk	.32 oz (9.0 g)	−cheeses	.10 to .55 oz (3–6 g)
−unsweetened condensed milk	.25 oz (7.0 g)		

2) Plant and protein sources

−soy	1.25 oz (35.0 g)	−beans (red cooked)	.30 oz (8.0 g)
−wheat germ	.93 oz (26.0 g)	−chestnuts	.30 oz (8.0 g)
−spirulin (algae)	.90 oz (25.0 g)	−rice (cooked)	.30 oz (8.0 g)
−grilled salted peanuts	.90 oz (25.0 g)	−bread (white)	.25 oz (7.0 g)
−almonds	.65 oz (19.0 g)	−lentils (cooked)	.85 oz (24.0 g)
−oats	.50 oz (14.0 g)	−white beans (cooked)	.75 oz (21.0 g)
−rye bread	.45 oz (13.0 g)	−chick peas	.20 oz (6.0 g)
−wheat bread	.42 oz (12.0 g)	−cocoa (powder)	.60 oz (17.0 g)
−barley	.40 oz (11.5 g)	−whole wheat noodles	.30 oz (8.0 g)
−walnuts	.36 oz (10.2 g)	−white flour noodles	.10 oz (3.0 g)
−corn	.32 oz (9.0 g)	−potatoes (cooked)	.07 oz (2.0 g)
		−chocolate	.30 oz (8.0 g)

C) PROTEINS' FOOD VALUES

Except for the egg, the different animal and vegetable proteins do not contain the necessary balance of amino acids. If one amino acid is missing, it can constitute a limiting factor which can impede the assimilation of other amino acids. Therefore, animal and vegetable proteins must be combined in the diet to create this needed balance.

A diet made up exclusively of vegetable amino acids is not considered a balanced diet as it lacks cysteine. This deficiency can cause hair and nail problems.

Similarly, a protein intake based solely on meat and fish will lead to a lack of lysine which can block the absorption of acids.

In order to obtain a proper protein intake, a balance must be struck:

–among essential amino acids,
–between the required amino acids and others,
–between vegetable and animal proteins,
–among proteins, vitamins A & C and trace elements.

D) **TO LOSE WEIGHT**

It is important to remember that proteins are crucial dietary elements. They do not cause weight gain and are even sometimes used in hospital weight-loss programs. They are even included in high-protein diets used to treat paradoxal obesity. What is important is the type of fats as well as the foods they are associated with in the diet.

BIBLIOGRAPHY

APFELBAUM M.,   *Diététique et nutrition* Ed. Masson 1989
FORRAT C.,
NILLUS P.
BRINGER J.,   *Evaluation de l'état nutritionnel protéique* Rev. Prat. 1985, 35, 3, 17–22

RICHARD J.L.,
MIROUZE J.
RUASSE J.P.   *Les composants de la matière vivante* Ed. L'indispensable en nutrition 1988
RUASSE J.P.   *Des protides, pourquoi, combien?* Ed. L'indispensable en nutrition 1987

CARBOHYDRATES

A) **INTRODUCTION**

Carbohydrates are ternary compounds (made up of carbon, hydrogen and oxygen). They are so called because their general formula is $Cn(H_2O)n$. This category covers monosaccharides (ie. simple sugars) that cannot be decomposed by hydrolysis, and polysaccharides, which on hydrolysis yield one or more monosaccharides.

B) GLYCEMIA

Glucose is the body's principle fuel. It is stored in the form of glycogen in the muscles and the liver. Glycemia is the amount of glucose in the blood; on an empty stomach the usual glycemic level is 5.5mmol/l or 1 g/l.

After a carbohydrate has been absorbed on an empty stomach, the blood sugar levels vary as follows:

-first, glycemia increases (according to the type of carbohydrate consumed);
-second, insulin is secreted by the pancreas; this causes the glycemic level to decrease once the glucose has entered the cells;
-third, glycemia reverts back to its normal level of 5.5 mmol/l.

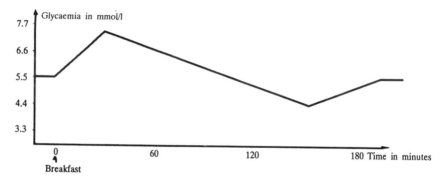

C) CARBOHYDRATES AND THEIR CHEMICAL FORMULAE

1) Simple sugars (or oligosaccharides)

These are composed of one molecule. They include:
-glucose (in fruits, honey, corn, wheat)
-fructose (in fruits, honey)
-galactose (in milk)

2) Disaccharides

These are composed of two simple sugar molecules. They include:
-saccharose (glucose + fructose) is extracted from beets or sugar cane. Saccharose is also found in carrots and fruits.
-lactose (glucose + galactose), the sugar in mammal's milk.
-maltose (glucose + glucose), a malt extract, which is the sugar in beer.

3) Polysaccharides

-glycogen from liver
-starch, in which the molecule contains about 200 glucose molecules. It is found in all starchy foods:

Cereals	wheat (flour, bread, semolina, pasta)	Grains	peas
	corn (popcorn, cornflakes)		chick peas
	rice		white beans
Tubers	potatoes		lentils
Roots	rutabaga		peanuts

The above classification was long the basis for the theory that since oligosaccharides and disaccharides have a simple molecular structure, they demanded only limited intestinal processing, and were thus, rapidly absorbed in the small intestine. They were consequently named "quick sugars".

Conversely, polysaccharides, made up of starches with more than 200 glucose molecules, were thought to require a long hydrolysis due to their complex molecular structure. Their absorption was believed to take longer. They were named "slow sugars".

In fact, this categorization was purely theoretical. The glycemic peak for all carbohydrates, both "quick" and "slow", taken individually on an empty stomach, occur at almost the same time, 20 to 25 minutes after initial ingestion.

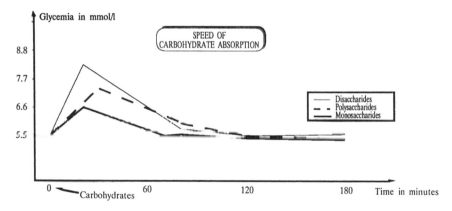

However, when several types are eaten together, for example in a meal, the absorption rate depends on:
- the type of food
- how it was prepared
- the caloric value of the meal
- the meal composition: the presence of fiber or proteins slows down starch digestion
- how quickly the gastro-intestinal tract is emptied (this process is faster for liquids).

169

D) GLYCEMIC INDEX

Rather than being concerned with absorption speed, it is more germane to study carbohydrates in terms of the glycemic increase they can induce.

The level of blood sugar increase caused by ingesting a given carbohydrate is defined by the glycemic index established by Dr. P.A. Crapo in 1976. The glycemic level corresponds to the triangular surface area under the blood sugar curve induced by the food tested. Glucose is arbitrarily given a rating of 100. The index of other foods is calculated using the formula:

$$\frac{\text{triangle surface area for the food tested}}{\text{triangle surface area for glucose}} \times 100$$

The higher the blood sugar increase induced by the tested carbohydrate, the higher the glycemic index.

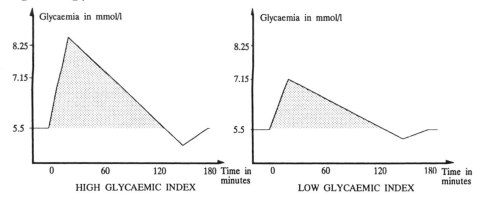

Glycemic index for different carbohydrates:

Maltose	110	Whole wheat bread	50
Glucose	100	Oatmeal	50
White bread	95	Whole wheat pasta	45
Instant mashed potatoes	95	Fresh white beans	40
Highly refined sugar	95	Whole rye bread	40
Honey, jam	90	Green peas	40
Cornflakes	85	Whole grain cereal	35
Carrots	85	Multi-grain bread	35
White sugar	75	Milk products	35
Corn	70	Fresh fruits	35
French bread	70	Wild rice	35
White rice	70	Lentils	30
Beets	70	Chick peas	30
Cookies	70	Milk	30

Boiled potatoes	70	Dried beans	30
Pasta	65	Dark chocolate	22
Sherbet	65	Fructose	20
Banana	60	Soy	15
Grapes	60	Peanuts	15
Bran cereal	50	Green vegetables	<15
Brown rice	50		

It is imperative to keep in mind that chemical processing of foods increases their glycemic index (cornflakes = 85 whereas corn = 70; instant mashed potatoes = 95 whereas boiled potatoes = 70).

When the glycemic index is equal to or greater than 60, the initial glycemic peak favors hyperinsulinism. In order to simplify matters, carbohydrates in this category are called "bad carbohydrates". On the other hand, the other carbohydrates, whose glycemic indices are inferior to 50, are due to "good carbohydrates".

Just as chemical processing increases a food's glycemic index, foods consumed in their natural state have a low glycemic index. Whole grain cereals and whole wheat breads containing fiber, vitamins and trace elements, are quite effective in lowering the body's blood sugar peaks.

Composition of 100 g or 3.5 ounces of wheat flour:

	whole wheat flour Ounces Grams	refined white flour Ounces Grams
proteins	.49 oz (14.0 g)	.330 oz (9.6 g)
fats	.07 oz (2.0 g)	.035 oz (1.0 g)
carbohydrates	2.54 oz (72.0 g)	2.680 oz (0.3 g)
fibers	.40 oz (11.9 g)	.010 oz (0.3 g)
	Milligrams	
calcium	41.0 mg	16.0 mg
phosphorous	370.0 mg	87.0 mg
magnesium	90.0 mg	25.0 mg
iron	3.3 mg	0.8 mg
Vitamin B1	550.0 mg	63.0 mg
Vitamin B2	116.0 mg	
	43.0 mg	

A comparative study of the glycemic effect and insulin levels after absorption by healthy subjects and non-insulino-dependant diabetics of whole wheat or refined flour gave the following results:

171

	whole wheat flour	refined white flour
Healthy subjects –Glycemia triangle –surface area (mmol/l/mn)	93	141
–Insulinemia triangle –surface area (mU/l/mn)	3,095	3,992
Diabetic subjects –Glycemia triangle –surface area (mmol/l/mn)	553	683
–Insulinemia triangle –surface area (mmol/l/mn)	3,397	4,157

The presence of fibers in whole wheat flour helps diminish blood sugar and insulin peaks.

The following graph shows that the glycemic peak is lower for brown rice than it is for white rice. As the degree of processing of a carbohydrate increases, so does the glycemic peak it causes.

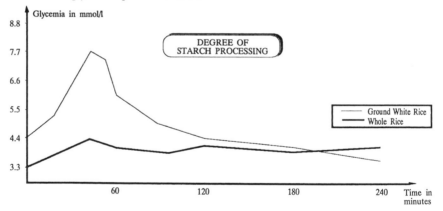

Moreover:

–the glycemic index rises when foods are cooked.
–the glycemic index lowers during a balanced meal. For example, the glycemic index is 65 for spaghetti alone, but drops to 30 if the pasta is absorbed as part of a balanced meal. The speed with which the gastro-intestinal tract empties is slower because of the presence of proteins and fats.

In fact, when a carbohydrate is absorbed, it produces an insulin peak that is even stronger than the glycemic peak. An index of blood insulin levels should be established to help obese persons determine which carbohydrates they can most safely consume.

E) GLYCONEOGENESIS

Glucose is produced from carbohydrates. However, glucose from carbohydrates is not the body's only source of glycogen. The Krebs cycle is the key of the metabolism: the organism is capable of manufacturing glucose from amino acids or from fatty acids (a process called glyconeogenesis).

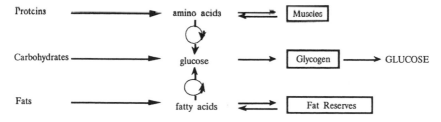

Taken to extremes, it could be assumed that the organism could survive without carbohydrates since it is capable of glyconeogenesis. Atkins took this extreme position by completely eliminating carbohydrates from his weight-loss method. However, the absence of carbohydrates, resulted in ketosis, causing metabolic disorders. In addition, Atkins made no distinction among the type of fat prescribed, so that his diet, too rich in fats, created an increased risk of cardiovascular disease.

The Montignac method avoids Atkins' error by preserving all carbohydrates with a low glycemic index in Phase I (weight-loss), and reintroducing carbohydrates with a medium glycemic index in Phase II (weight stabilization). Moreover, the method gives exact advice on the choice of fats.

From this explanation of the body's ability to produce sugar using carbohydrates, many parents will perhaps be better able to understand the error they may be committing when they give their children white sugar. Perhaps they believe it is important for their growth and development. They therefore ply their children with candy, cakes, and sugary soft drinks, and fail to realize that the ingestion of glucose is not necessary because the need for glucose can be fully satisfied through the ingestion of (good) carbohydrates which help ensure healthy growth and development.

BIBLIOGRAPHY

BANTLE J.P.,   *Post prandial glucose and insulin responses to meals containing*
LAINE D.C.   *different carbohydrates in normal and diabetic subjects* New
   Engl. J. Med. 1983, 309, 7–12

BORNET F.   *Place des glucides simples et des produits amylacés dans*
   l'alimentation des diabétiques en 1985. Fondation
   RONAC. Paris

CRAPO P.A.   *Plasma, glucose and insulin responses to orally administered*
   simple and complex carbohydrates Diabetes 1976, 25, 741–
   747

CRAPO P.A.   *Post prandial plasma, glucose and insulin response to different*
   complex carbohydrates Diabetes 1977, 26, 1178–1183

CRAPO P.A.   *Comparison of serum glucose-insulin and glucagon responses to*
   different types of carbohydrates in non-insulin dependent diabetic
   patients Am. J. Clin. Nutr. 1981, 34, 84–90

CHEW L.   *Applications of glycemic index to mixed meals* Am. J. Clin.
   Nutr. 1988, 47, 53–56

DANQUECHIN-   *Rôle de la phase gastrique de la digestion sur la biodisponibilité*
DORVAL E.   *des hydrates de carbone et leurs effets métaboliques* Journées
   de diabétologie de l'Hôtel-Dieu 1975

DESJEUX J.F.   *Glycémie, insuline et acides gras dans le plasma d'adolescents*
   sains après ingestion de bananes Med. et Nutr. 1982, 18,
   2, 127–130

FEWKES D.W.   *Sucrose* Science Progres 1971, 59, 25, 39

GABREAU T.,   *Les modifications de la vitesse d'absorption des glucides* Med.
LEBLANC H.   et Nutr. 1983, XIX, 6, 447–449

GUILLAUSSEAU P.J.,   *Effet hyperglycémiant des aliments* Gaz. Med. Fr. 1989, 96,
GUILLAUSSEAU-   30, 61–63
SCHOLER C.

HEATON K.W.   *Particule size of wheat, maize and oat test meals: effects on*
   plasma, glucose and insulin responses and on the rate of starch
   digestion in vitro Am. J. Clin. Nutr. 1988, 47, 675–682

HERAUD G.   *Glucides simples, glucides complexes*
HODORA D.   *Glucides simples, glucides complexes et glucides indigestibles*
   Gaz. Med. Fr. 1981, 88, 37, 5, 255–259

JENKINS D.J.A.   *Glycemic index of foods: a physiological basis for carbohydrates*
   exchange Am. J. Clin. Nutr. 1981, 34, 362–366

JENKINS D.J.A.   *Dietary carbohydrates and their glycemic responses* J.A.M.A.
   1984, 2, 388–391

JENKINS D.J.A.   *Wholemeal versus wholegrain breads: proportion of whole or*
   cracked grains and the glycemic response Br Med. J. 1988,
   297, 958–960

JIAN R. *La vidange d'un repas ordinaire chez l'homme: étude par la méthode radio-isotopique* Nouv. Presse Med. 1979, 8, 667–671

KERIN O'DEA *Physical factor influencing post prandial glucose and insulin responses to starch* Am. J. Clin. Nutr. 1980, 33, 760–765

NATHAN D. *Ice-cream in the diet of insulin-dependent diabetic patients* J.A.M.A. 1984, 251, 21, 2825–2827

NICOLAIDIS S. *Mode d'action des substances de goût sucré sur le métabolisme et sur la prise alimentaire. Les sucres dans l'alimentation* Cool. Sc. Fond. Fr. Nutr. 1981

NOUROT J. *Relationship between the rate of gastric emptying and glucose insulin responses to starchy food in young healthy adults* Am. J. Clin. Nutr. 1988, 48, 1035–1040

O'DONNELL L.J.D. *Size of flour particles and its relation to glycemia, insulinoemia and calonic disease.* Br. Med. J. 17 June 1984, 298, 115–116

REAVEN C. *Effects of source of dietary carbohydrates on plasma, glucose and insulin to test meals in normal subjects* Am J. Clin. Nutr. 1980, 33, 1279–1283

ROUX E. *Index glycémique* Gaz. Med. Fr. 1988, 95, 18, 77–78

RUASSE J.P. *Des glucides, pourquoi, comment?* Collection «L'indispensable en nutrition» 1987

SCHLIENGER J.L. *Signification d'une courbe d'hyperglycémie orale plate; comparaison avec un repas d'épreuve* Nouv. Pr. Med. 1982, 52, 3856–3857

SLAMA G. *Correlation between the nature of amount of carbohydrates in intake and insulin delivery by the artificial pancreas in 24 insulin-dependent diabetics* Diabetes 1981, 30, 101–105

SLAMA G. *Sucrose taken during mixed meal has no additional hyperglycemic action over isocaloric amounts of starch in well-controlled diabetics* Lancet, 1984, 122–124

STACH J.K. *Contribution à l'étude d'une diététique rationnelle du diabétique: rythme circadien de la tolérance au glucose, intérêt du pain complet, intérêt du sorbitol.* Thèse pour le doctorat en Médecine, Caen 1974

THORBURN A.W. *The glycemic index of food* Med. J. Austr. May 26th 198? 144, 580–582

VAGUE P. *Influence comparée des différents glucides alimentaires sur la sécrétion hormonale. Les sucres dans l'alimentation.* Collection Scientifique de la Fondation Française pour la Nutrition

FATS

A) INTRODUCTION

Lipids or fats are indispensable to our diet because they:

–supply energy
–allow the constitution of fat reserves
–are required to build cellular membranes
–are part of the tissue and nervous system composition
–facilitate the synthesis of hormones, prostacyclins, thromboxanes and leukotrienes
–are the basis of the synthesis of biliary salts
–constitute the only source of so-called vital fatty acids, linoleic acid and alpha-linolenic acids
–contain the liposoluble vitamins, A, D, E, and K
–play a key role in cardiovascular pathology

Per capita, fat consumption in the American diet has increased between 1909 and 1985, reaching 169 grams or 6 oz per day in 1985. In the United States, the proportion of total fats from meat, poultry, and fish has changed only slightly, reaching 31.4 percent in 1985. The relative amount of fat from whole milk has declined steadily from a high of 10.4 percent in 1947–49 to 3 percent in 1985, while the ratio from fats and oils has increased from 38 percent to 47 percent in the same period. (Nutrition Monitoring in the United States: An Update Report on Nutrition Monitoring, pg. 52).

B) LIPID BIOCHEMISTRY

Fat compounds are composed of 98% triglycerides. Triglycerides are produced by linking three fatty acid molecules (hence the prefix "tri") onto a glycerol molecule, which is, in fact, an alcohol. The remaining two percent of fat are phospholipids (especially lecithin), sterols (including cholesterol and ergosterol) and liposoluble vitamins.

A fatty acid is made of a long chain of carbon atoms, to which hydrogen atoms are attached. There are three types of fatty acids: saturated fatty acids and mono and polyunsaturated fatty acids. Sometimes the carbon atoms are connected by a double bond.

–If there is no double bond, the fatty acids are saturated. The saturated fatty acids most commonly found in foods are lauric, myristic, palmitic and stearic acids.
–If there is only one double bond, the fatty acid is mono-unsaturated; the most common type is oleic acid.
–If there is more than one double bond, the fatty acids are polyunsaturated; linoleic acid and alpha-linolenic acid are the most important types. They must be obtained through food because the body is not capable of synthesizing them independently.

C) INDISPENSABLE FATTY ACIDS

These are polyunsaturated fatty acids:

1) Linoleic acid (C 18 : 2n–6 or omega 6):

Linoleic acid is found in sunflower oil, corn oil and grape seed oil. It is part of the cellular membrane, and the messages transmitted through the nervous system are dependent upon its availability. It neutralizes free carcinogenic radicles, preventing the development of skin cancer in mice, for example.

  –It is a precursor of prostaglandines and prostacyclines.
  –It limits the ability of platelet aggregation and helps reduce blood pressure.
  –A deficiency in linoleic acid causes:
  • growth problems
  • cellular modifications in the skin, mucous membranes, endocrine glands and genitals
  • mitochondria dysfunctions
  • anomalies in the transportation of blood lipids
  –The recommended intake is .90 ounces (25 g) per day. This quantity can be obtained by consuming:
  • 1.2 oz of sunflower oil (35 g)
  • 1.3 oz of walnut oil (37 g)
  • 1.5 oz of corn oil (45 g)
  • 1.8 oz of soy oil (50 g)
  • 1.9 oz of safflower margarine (55 g)
  • 2.9 oz of peanut oil (83 g)

2) Alpha-linolenic acid (C 18 : 3n-3 or omega 3).

  –This acid is especially found in walnut oil, soy oil, wheat germ, lecithin and algae. Little is found in peanut oil, sunflower oil, corn oil or grape seed oil.
  –A deficiency in alpha-linolenic acid causes:
  • structural anomalies of cellular membranes
  • a malfunctioning of the retina when stimulated by light
  • learning difficulties
  • lowered alcohol tolerance
  • anomalies of the nervous transmission due to a loss of ionic equilibrium. (It diminishes the Na-K ATPase's activity by half).
  –The body requires .07 to .11 ounces (2 to 3 g) per day.
  –Amount of alpha-linolenic acid in 3.5 ounces (100 g) of oil:
  • soy oil: .21   ounces (6.0 g)
  • corn oil: .032 ounces (0.9 g)
  • peanut oil: .028 ounces (0.8 g)
  • olive oil: .018 ounces (0.5 g)
  • safflower oil: .018 ounces (0.5 g)
  • grape seed oil: .018 ounces (0.5 g)

3) Arachidonic acid (C 20 : 4n–6)

Arachidonic acid is also considered indispensable because the body sometimes has difficulties in synthesizing it from linoleic acid.

It is present in animal fats. It is necessary in the formation of type 2 icosanoids which play a major role in preventing inflammations.

D) FAT SOURCES

Fats are found in animal tissues and in plants.

1) Animal fats:

Quantity of lipids in 3.5 ounces (100 g) of food:

Meats
- Beef: .14–.90 oz (4–25 g)

Meats		
• Beef: .14–.90 oz (4–25 g)	–steak or roast:	.14 oz (4.0 g)
	–neck:	.24 oz (7.0 g)
	–ribs:	.45 oz (13.0 g)
	–shin:	.70 oz (20.0 g)
	–hamburger:	.90 oz (25.0 g)
• Veal: .07–.50 oz (2–15 g)	–brains:	.31 oz (9.0 g)
	–filet:	.35 oz (10.0 g)
	–ribs:	.50 oz (15.0 g)
• Pork: .07–.50 oz (2–15 g)	–shoulder:	.24 oz (7.0 g)
	–chops:	.90 oz (25.0 g)
	–roast:	.90 oz (25.0 g)
• Lamb: .17–1.0 oz (5–30 g)	–leg:	.56 oz (16.0 g)
	–neck:	.60 oz (17.0 g)
	–shoulder:	.90 oz (25.0 g)
	–chops:	.90 oz (25.0 g)
Cold Cuts	–lean ham, sweetbreads, bacon, roast pork	.32 oz (9.0 g)
	–dry ham, tripe sausages, headcheese	.35–.70 oz (10–20 g)
	–sausages	.70–1.00 oz (20–30 g)
	–dry sausages	1.00–1.40 oz (30–40 g)
	–bacon bits	2.500 oz (70.0 g)
Eggs	–whole eggs	.350 oz (10.0 g)
	–albumen (white)	0 oz (0.0 g)
	–yolk	1.200 oz (33.0 g)
Poultry	–chicken without skin	.240 oz (7.0 g)
	–chicken with skin	.420 oz (12.0 g)
	–duck	.350 oz (10.0 g)
	–rabbit	.350 oz (10.0 g)
	–chicken	1.000 oz (30.0 g)
Dairy Products	–skim milk	.003 oz (0.1 g)

	–low-fat milk	.060 oz (1.7 g)
	–whole milk	.120 oz (3.5 g)
	–sweetened condensed milk	.350 oz (10.0 g)
Cheese	–non-fat cottage cheese	0 oz (0.0 g)
	–cottage cheese (40% fat)	.350 oz (10.0 g)
	–cottage cheese (60% fat)	.450 oz (18.0 g)
	–plain yogurt	.050 oz (1.5 g)
	–low-fat yogurt	.003 oz (0.1 g)
	–cheese spread	.770 oz (22.0 g)
	–Swiss	1.100 oz (32.0 g)
	–blue, roquefort	1.200 oz (34.0 g)
Fish	–lean fish: sole, coal fish, ray fish	.070 oz (2.0 g)
	–semi-fat fish: sardines, herring, salmon	.14–.30 oz (4–8 g)
	–fatty fish: mackerel, tuna	.35–.50 oz (10–15 g)
Shellfish	–crab	.070 oz (2.0 g)
	–shrimp	.100 oz (3.0 g)
	–oysters	.070 oz (2.0 g)
	–mussels	.070 oz (2.0 g)
	–scallops	.035 oz (1.0 g)

2) Vegetable fats:

–Peanuts	–Walnuts
–Corn	–Soy
–Sunflower	–Copra
–Grape seeds	–Palm

E) FATS AS COMPONENTS OF FOODS

1) Virtually pure fats

–Oils:	3.5 oz of lipids for 3.5 oz of food
	100 g of lipids for 100 g of food
–Lard:	3.60 oz (94.0 g)
–Butter:	2.85 oz (81.0 g)
–Margarine:	2.90 oz (82.5 g)
–Light butter:	1.48 oz (42.0 g)
–Cream (30% fat):	1.00 oz (30.0 g)

2) Fat-Protein Associations

–Meat	–Shellfish
–Cold cuts	–Milk, dairy products
–Eggs	–Cheese
–Fish	

179

3) Fat-Carbohydrate Associations

	Carbohydrates	Fats		Carbohydrates	Fats
−Liver	.14 oz (4.0 g)	.17 oz (5.0 g)	−Black olives	.95 oz (27.0 g)	1.30 oz (36.0 g)
−Breaded fish	.25 oz (7.0 g)	.32 oz (9.0 g)	−Avocados	.17 oz (5.0 g)	.60 oz (17.0 g)
−Oysters	.14 oz (4.0 g)	.07 oz (2.0 g)	−Soy	1.10 oz (32.0 g)	.60 oz (17.0 g)
−Scallops	.10 oz (3.0 g)	.03 oz (1.0 g)	−Pasta with eggs	.85 oz (2.4 g)	.07 oz (2.0 g)
−Milk	.17 oz (3.0 g)	.12 oz (3.5 g)	−Fries, chips	1.80 oz (50.0 g)	1.40 oz (40.0 g)
−Condensed milk	1.20 oz (34.0 g)	.35 oz (10.0 g)	−Coconut	2.00 oz (60.0 g)	.25 oz (7.0 g)
−Powdered soup	1.90 oz (55.0 g)	.40 oz (11.0 g)	−Chestnuts pureed	.30 oz (1.0 g)	1.40 oz (40.0 g)
−Sauces with flour	1.80 oz (50.0 g)	.42 oz (12.0 g)	−Dark chocolate	1.90 oz (55.0 g)	.95 oz (27.0 g)
−Walnuts	1.70 oz (5.0 g)	1.80 oz (50.0 g)	−Crackers	2.40 oz (75.0 g)	.14 oz (4.0 g)
−Almonds	.50 oz (15.0 g)	1.90 oz (55.0 g)	−Ice cream	.90 oz (25.0 g)	.25 oz (7.0 g)
−Roasted salted peanuts	.70 oz (20.0 g)	1.80 oz (50.0 g)	−Apple pie	.93 oz (28.0 g)	.30 oz (8.0 g)
			−Waffles	2.30 oz (73.0 g)	.70 oz (20.0 g)

F) FATS AND THEIR IMPACT ON CHOLESTEROL

1) Saturated fatty acids

These acids increase the cholesterol level, particularly those found in meats, cold cuts, milk, dairy products and cheese.

So, to a lesser extent, do the acids found in eggs, poultry without skin and shellfish.

2) Mono and polyunsaturated fatty acids help lower the cholesterol level

a) Monounsaturated fatty acids are found in olive oil.
b) Polyunsaturated fatty acids of vegetable origin are found in sunflower oil, corn oil, grape seed oil, and peanut oil.
c) Polyunsaturated fatty acids from animal sources are found in fish oils.

G) FAT CONSUMPTION

The recommended daily averages are:

−2.45 to 2.80 oz for men (70 to 80 g)
−2.1 to 2.8 oz for women (60 to 80 g)

Today, the average daily consumption comprises approximately:

−60% saturated fatty acids
−33% monounsaturated fatty acids
−7% polyunsaturated fatty acids

180

To prevent cardiovascular disease, the World Health Organization recommends the following distribution:

-25% saturated fatty acids
-25% monounsaturated fatty acids
-50% polyunsaturated fatty acids.

It is therefore imperative to implement this consumption pattern by eating more fish, decreasing meat consumption, and by broadening the range of vegetable oils we eat.

BIBLIOGRAPHY

BOURRE J.M.- *The importance of dietary linoeic acid in composition of nervous membranes.*

DURAND G. Diet and life style, new technology De M.F. Mayol 1988 John Libbey Eurotext Ldt p. 477–481

DYERBERG J. *Linolenic acid and eicospentaenoic acid* The Lancet 26 Janvier 1980, p. 199

JACOTOT B. *Olive oil and the lipoprotein metabolism.* Rev. Fr. des Corps Gras 1988, 2, 51–55

MAILLARD C. *Graisses grises* Gazette Med. de Fr. 1989, 96, n° 22

RUASSE J.P. *Des lipides, pourquoi, comment?* Coll. L'Indispensable en Nutrition.

VLES R.O. *Connaissances récentes sur les effets physiologiques des margarines riches en acide linoléique.* Rev. Fr. des Corps Gras 1980, 3, 115–120

Documentation Astra-Calvé:
L'essential sur les acides gras polyinsaturés
Lipides et santé. Quelles vérités?
Connaissance des corps gras.
Mémento des corps gras.

DIETARY FIBERS

A) WHAT IS FIBER?

Dietary fiber is sometimes classified as indigestible carbohydrates. However, it can actually be defined as plant cell residues, resistant to the enzyme action of the small intestine, but which is, nonetheless, partially hydrolyzed by colic bacterial flora.

B) THE MAIN FIBER TYPES

They include:
−cellulose	−pectin
−hemicellulose	−gums
−lignin	

C) WHERE FIBER IS FOUND

Fibers are found in cereals, fresh vegetables and legumes, fruits and algae.

Cereals contain:	−cellulose	−some pectin
	−hemicellulose	−bran cereal has a fiber
	−lignin	content of 50% while white flour contains 3% fiber
Fresh vegetables contain:	−cellulose	−some lignin
	−hemicellulose	
	−pectin	
Dried legumes contain:	−cellulose	−gums
	−hemicellulose	−some lignin
	−pectin	
Fruits contain:	−cellulose	−lignin
	−hemicellulose	−pectin
Algae contains:	−agar	−alginates
	−carraghcnates	−gums

D) DAILY RATION OF FIBERS

The recommended daily fiber intake is 1.4 oz in the United States, however, the average person is far below this daily recommended allowance (RDA). Estimates of mean daily dietary fiber intake over a four-day period from the CSFII 1985–86 are .39 oz for women aged 20–49 years and .35 oz for children aged 1–5 years. This survey showed that only five percent of the women surveyed had intakes of .7 oz or more of dietary fiber per day. One-day data from the CSFII 1985 indicated that on average the dietary fiber intake of men is higher than that of women (approximately .6 oz per day). (Nutrition Monitoring in the United States: An Update Report on Nutrition Monitoring, 1989, pg. 54).

It is worth noting that .60 oz of bran contain as much fiber as 24.5 oz of carrots or 52.5 oz of apples.

E) FIBER SOURCES AND FIBER CONTENT PER 3.5 oz (100 g) OF FOOD

		Ounces	*Grams*		*Ounces*	*Grams*
Cereal products	–bran	1.40 oz	(40.0 g)	–brown rice	.17 oz	(5.0 g)
	–whole wheat flour	.35 oz	(10.0 g)	–white bread	.035 oz	(1.0 g)
	–whole wheat bread	.31 oz	(9.0 g)	–white rice	.035 oz	(1.0 g)
	–whole grain bread	.17 oz	(5.0 g)			
Dried legumes:	–beans	.90 oz	(25.0 g)	–lentils	.42 oz	(12.0 g)
	–split peas	.80 oz	(23.0 g)	–chick peas	.07 oz	(2.0 g)
Dried fruits and nuts	–dry coconut	.85 oz	(24.0 g)	–prunes	.25 oz	(7.0 g)
(Oil-rich vegetable	–dry figs	.63 oz	(18.0 g)	–raisins	.25 oz	(7.0 g)
products)	–almonds	.48 oz	(14.0 g)	–cocoa	.20 oz	(6.0 g)
	–dates	.32 oz	(9.0 g)	–walnuts	.17 oz	(5.0 g)
	–peanuts	.30 oz	(8.0 g)	–olives	.17 oz	(5.0 g)
Fresh fruits:	–raspberries	.30 oz	(8.0 g)	–strawberries	.07 oz	(2.0 g)
	–currants	.25 oz	(7.0 g)	–oranges	.07 oz	(2.0 g)
	–pears with skin	.10 oz	(3.0 g)	–cantaloupe	.07 oz	(2.0 g)
	–apples with skin	.10 oz	(3.0 g)	–grapes	.035 oz	(1.0 g)
	–peaches	.07 oz	(2.0 g)			
Fresh vegetables:	–cooked peas	.42 oz	(12.0 g)	–cabbage	.14 oz	(4.0 g)
	–parsley	.32 oz	(9.0 g)	–green beans	.07 oz	(2.0 g)
	–cooked spinach	.25 oz	(7.0 g)	–eggplant	.07 oz	(2.0 g)
	–canned peas	.20 oz	(6.0 g)	–zucchini	.07 oz	(2.0 g)
	–dandelion greens	.17 oz	(5.0 g)	–carrots	.07 oz	(2.0 g)
	–artichokes	.14 oz	(4.0 g)	–lettuce	.07 oz	(2.0 g)

F) PHYSIOLOGICAL EFFECTS OF FIBERS

–They stimulate salivary and gastric secretions.
–They fill the stomach, creating the sensation of having eaten enough.
–They delay the emptying of the gastrointestinal tract.
–They foster bile salt secretion which is necessary to digest fats.
–They ensure regularity in the colon.
–They increase the volume and moisture content of the feces, which helps prevent constipation.

G) ACTION OF FIBERS IN PATHOLOGICAL CASES

1) Obesity

Some fibers, especially when consumed raw, form a thick hydrophilic gel which coats the walls of the gastrointestinal tract. This gel slows down the emptying of the gastrointestinal tract, thereby creating a type of filter that limits carbohydrate absorption. The energy absorbed from sugars is then reduced and post-prandial hyperglycemic peaks are avoided. This effect is especially apparent with pectin and gum.

One of the greatest problems of obese individuals is hyperinsulinism and insulin resistance. These disorders are caused by hyperglycemic peaks induced by the consumption of certain carbohydrates. Pectin and gums are fibers that counteract these effects.

–Pectin is found in fruits (especially apples), peas and dried beans.
–An apple contains .44 oz of usable carbohydrates and .087 oz of fiber (pectin and cellulose).

Holt's experiments show that .48 oz of pectin considerably reduce the glycemic reaction after the ingestion of 1.75 oz of glucose.

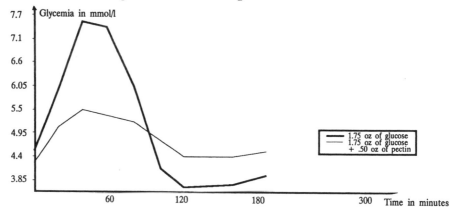

–Gums:

The most widely used gum is guar gum, an industrial derivative of an Indian bean. There is also some gum content in vegetables and oats.

Tagliafero clearly demonstrates the effect of .30 oz (8 g) of gum per day, taken in two doses, on glycemic and insulinemic levels following injections of glucose.

	Without Gums	With Gums
Glycemia	7.25 ± 0.05	6.75 ± 0.03
Insulinemia	13 ± 3	$10 \pm 1,5$

Guar gum improves peripheral sensitivity to insulin and reduces insulin resistance. By smoothing out post-prandial glycemic peaks, it reduces stimulation of the pancreatic B-cells.

Jenkins shows that a daily intake of .51 oz of guar gum eliminates any glycemic peak after meals and reduces insulin secretion by more than 50%.

Monnier's experiments demonstrate that the addition of fiber in the diet diminishes the post-prandial hyperglycemic reaction:

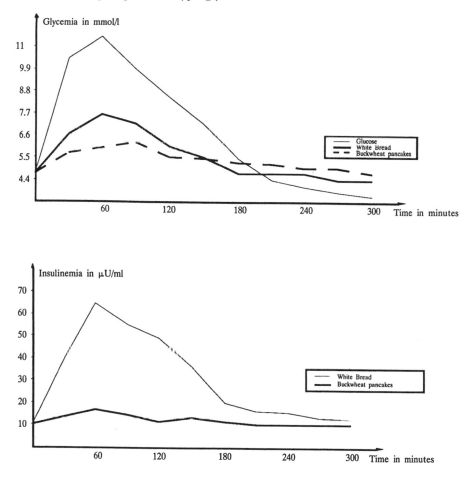

The insulinic response is in part induced and stimulated by the entero-hormonal system (gastric inhibitory polypeptides GIP) and entero-glucagon.

Increased dietary fiber consumption contributes to a reduction of the GIP and entero-glucagon responses. Moreover, fibers are accountable for the disappearance of reactionary hypoglycemia due to either a decrease in the insulinic effect or the reactivation of pancreatic glucagon secretion three hours following the beginning of the alimentary intake.

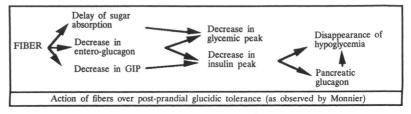

Action of fibers over post-prandial glucidic tolerance (as observed by Monnier)

2) **In Diabetic Cases**

The same beneficial effects for diabetics are found in terms of glucidic tolerance. Miranda proved that .70 oz of fiber can decrease a diabetic's glycemia from 57% to 13%.

3) **Hypercholesterolemia**

As we will see later, fiber also improves cholesterol levels. Anderson has given a number of hypotheses on this subject:

Soluble fibers bind to bile acids and interfere with the formation of micelles in the proximal ileum. This binding process diminishes the quantity of cholesterol and fatty acids absorbed and/or modifies the size of lipoproteinic molecules formed by the intestinal mucosa.

Soluble fibers increase fecal excretion of bile acids and block the hepatic synthesis of lipoproteins.

Soluble fibers undergo colic fermentation by bacteria, producing gases and short-chain fatty acids which enter the portal circulation. This modifies hepatic synthesis of cholesterol.

4) **Digestive Problems**

Fibers
  - treat constipation
  - relieve spasmodic colitis
  - prevent cholesterolic vesicular lithiases, colic diverticulosis, and colon and rectal cancers.

BIBLIOGRAPHY

«Council Scientific Affairs».   *Fibres alimentaires et santé* JAMA 1984, 14, 190, 1037–1046

ANDERSON J.W.   *Dietary fiber: diabetes and obesity* Am. J. Gastroenterology 1986, 81, 898–906

BERNIER J.J.	*Fibres alimentaires, motricité et absorption intestinale. Effets sur l'hyperglycémie post-prandiale* Journée de Diabétologie Hôtel-Dieu 1979, 269–273
HABER G.B.	*Depletion and disruption of dietary fiber. Effects on satiety, plasma, glucose and serum insulin.* Lancet 1977, 2, 679–682
HEATON K.W.	*Food fiber as an obstacle to energy intake* Lancet 1973, 2, 1418–1421
HEATON K.W.	*Dietary fiber in perspective* Humon Clin. Nutr. 1983, 37c, 151–170
HOLT S.	*Effect of gel fiber on gastric emptying and absorption of glucose and paracetamol* Lancet 1979, March 24, 636–639
JENKINS D.J.A.	*Decrease in post-prandial insulin and glucose concentration by guar and pectin* Ann. Int. Med. 1977, 86, 20–33
JENKINS D.J.A.	*Dietary fiber, fiber analogues and glucose tolerance: importance of viscosity* Br Med. J. 1978, 1, 1392–1394
LAURENT B.	*Etudes récentes concernant les fibres alimentaires* Med. et Nutr. 1983, XIX, 2, 95–122
MONNIER L.	*Effets des fibres sur le métasbolisme glucidique* Cah. Nutr. Diet. 1983, XVIII, 89–93
NAUSS K.M.	*Dietary fat and fiber: relationship to caloric intake body growth, and colon carcinogenesis* Am. J. Clin. Nutr. 1987, 45, 243–251
SAUTIER C.	*Valeur alimentaire des algues spirulines chez l'Homme* Ann. Nutr. Alim. 1975, 29, 517
SAUTIER C.	*Les algues en alimentation humaine* Cah. Nutr. Diet, 1987, 6, 469–472

HYPERCHOLESTEROLEMIA CARDIOVASCULAR DISEASE AND DIET

A) CARDIOVASCULAR DISEASE

In the United States, between 1950 and 1985, heart disease continued to be the leading cause of death, and cerebrovascular disease was the third most important cause; together, the two accounted for approximately one half of all deaths. Thus, despite the drop in mortality from these cardiovascular diseases in recent years, they remain major public health concerns. (Vital Statistics data NCHS, 1988).

Coronary heart disease and cerebrovascular disease have many causes: obesity, nicotinism, arterial high blood pressure, diabetes and hypercholesterolemia.

Complications generally appear after the risk factors have accumulated, approximately 20 to 30 years later. However, to prevent diseases, early detection is important since a number of hereditary diseases can cause premature death: four percent of the deaths caused by cardiovascular disease occur between the ages of 15 and 24!

B) CHOLESTEROL

Cholesterol is not an intruder in the body: the organism contains approximately 3.5 oz (100 g) of cholesterol to be found in the central nervous system, in the myelin surrounding nerves, in cellular membranes and in circulating molecules.

It is indispensable to hormonal synthesis in the adrenal glands, ovaries and testicles.

The cholesterol found in the blood (blood cholesterol) can, of course, come from food, but most circulating cholesterol is made by the organism itself. For example, 12 to 800 to 1000 mg per day is released with bile in the small intestine.

Cholesterol is found not only in the blood, but also bound to proteins. There are two types of proteins found in the blood: Low-Density Lipoproteins (LDL) and High-Density Lipoproteins (HDL). Low-Density Lipoproteins (LDL) distribute the cholesterol to the cells, and in particular, to the arterial walls which are the victims of fat deposits. Hence the name "bad cholesterol" is responsible for coating and clogging the vessel walls.

The resulting obstruction of the arteries can cause:

–arteritis in the lower limbs
–angina pectoris or coronary thrombosis
–cerebrovascular incidents which can possibly result in paralysis

High-Density Lipoproteins (HDL) carry the cholesterol to the liver, where it is eliminated. No vascular deposits are formed. Hence the name "good cholesterol" attributed to HDL-cholesterol since it removes atheromatous deposits from the arteries. When HDL levels are high, the danger of a cardiovascular incident is reduced.

C) BLOOD CHOLESTEROL LEVELS

The current standards for blood cholesterol levels are far more stringent than those applied a few years ago.

Usually, the total cholesterol level should be less than or equal to 5.16 mmol/l.

–the LDL-cholesterol level should be less than 3.35 mmol/l.

–the HDL-cholesterol level should be greater than 1.16 mmol/l for men, and greater than 1.41 mmol/l for women.

In borderline cases, the purely protein part of the lipoproteins is also measured:

–the apolipoprotein A1 level (related to HDL-cholesterol) level should be greater than .04 oz per quart (1.30 g/l).
–the apolipoprotein B level (related to LDL-cholesterol) level should be greater than .015 oz per quart for men, and greater than .019 oz per quart for women.

The triglyceride level is affected by consumption of carbohydrates and alcohol, instead of fats. It should also be carefully watched. This level should be less than or equal to 1.72 mmol/l.

D) CARDIOVASCULAR RISKS

Cardiovascular risks increase twofold if the cholesterol level increases from 4.64 to 5.67 mmol/l, and become four times as great if the cholesterol level is higher than 6.7 mmol/l.

The average serum cholesterol level in the United States observed in 1980 and 1982 was the following:

Serum Cholesterol

	Ethnic Origin 50 years	Men Women 50 years
Mexican American	5.68 mmol/l	5.01 mmol/l
Cuban	5.65 mmol/l	5.98 mmol/l
Puerto Rican	5.82 mmol/l	5.96 mmol/l
White	5.92 mmol/l	6.30 mmol/l
Black	5.96 mmol/l	6.28 mmol/l

(Nutrition Monitoring in the United States: An Update Report on Nutrition Monitoring, 1989).

Lowering the total cholesterol level by 12.5% allows for a 19% decrease in the myocardial infarction rate and in the frequency of lethal myocardial ischemia.

However, measuring the total cholesterol level is not sufficient, as Ginsburg proved by showing that 15% of all myocardial infarction occurs in individuals whose total cholesterol level is between 3.87 and 5.16 mmol/l. Instead, it is important to measure the HDL-cholesterol level and calculate the total cholesterol level/HDL-cholesterol level quotient. This quotient should be lower than 4.5 mmol/l.

E) IMPROVED DIET

Alimentary precautions are sufficient for treating ordinary hypercholesterolemia (Fredericksen's type "IIA").

Medication is not always needed and should only be used as a second resort.

1) Weight-loss

Losing weight improves biological parameters in all cases.

To treat obesity, it is necessary to follow an adapted diet in order to bring weight back to normal.

2) Limit alimentary intake of cholesterol

Foods have varying cholesterol levels. For example, organ meats are very rich in cholesterol.

Cholesterol Milligrams

–2 1.75 oz eggs	600 mg	–beer yeast	700 mg
–3.5 oz egg yolk	1,500 mg	–shrimp	280 mg
–butter	250 mg	–fish	50–90 mg
–cheese		–meat, cold cuts,	
(30% butter fat)	100 mg	poultry	70 mg
–whole fat dairy			
products	80–100 mg		
–organ meats:			
.beef kidney	430 mg	.beef heart	175 mg
.veal kidney	400 mg	.veal tongue	90 mg
.beef liver	250 mg	.beef tongue	50 mg

The World Health Organization recommends a daily cholesterol intake of no more than 300 mg in order to avoid an increased cholesterol level.

However, recent studies have shown that this dietary aspect is only secondary. For example, a daily cholesterol intake of 1000 mg only increases the cholesterol level by approximately five percent.

Therefore, the cholesterol quantity in food can be ignored so long as the level of saturation of fatty acids is taken into consideration.

3) Therefore, fatty acids must be selected properly. More mono and polyunsaturated fatty acids should be consumed, and fewer saturated fats.

a) Saturated fatty acids

Saturated fatty acids are not recommended. They are found in meats, poultry, eggs, milk, dairy products and cheeses.

They increase the total cholesterol level, especially the LDL-cholesterol level. It is the LDL-cholesterol, as seen earlier, that is responsible for deposits on the arterial walls and cardiovascular disease.

However, a number of recent publications (Nutritional Reviews 1983, 41, #9 pp. 272–274) question these seemingly well-established facts. For example, although eggs are rich in saturated fatty acids, they do not seem to have the negative effects that they were accused of having. If three eggs are added to the daily diet of a group of 21 to 35 year old individuals, corresponding to a total daily ingestion (diet + eggs) of 975 mg of cholesterol (compared to 412 mg for the control group), no increase in the blood cholesterol level is observed!

The effect of poultry eaten without the skin, in terms of increasing the cholesterol level is low due to the corresponding low lipid level. This is also true for peanut oil. In this case, the effects of the saturated fatty acids are largely counterbalanced by the presence of polyunsaturated fatty acids.

b) Vegetable polyunsaturated fatty acids

Vegetable polyunsaturated fatty acids are found in sunflower oil, corn oil, grapeseed oil and rapeseed oil. Consuming these oils helps to lower both HDL and LDL-cholesterol, thereby reducing total cholesterol levels. Vegetable polyunsaturated fatty acids also contribute to limiting platelet aggregation which cause clotting of the arteriothrombosis.

c) Animal polyunsaturated fatty acid consumption is recommended

Eicosapentaenoic acid (EPA) and docosahexaenoic acid (DHA) are the two primary animal polyunsaturated fatty acids. They are derivatives of the alpha-linolenic acid found in fish oils.

The Danish scientist, Dyerberg, observed that the Eskimos rarely suffer from cardiovascular disease. Is this an acquired or an inherited trait? Studies showed that the Eskimos who left Greenland to start a new life in Canada or the United States soon became victims of cardiovascular disease. Therefore, it is not an ethnic characteristic but rather an acquired trait directly linked to the Eskimos' rich fish diet in Greenland.

In 1985, a statistical study conducted over the course of 20 years was published in the "New England Journal of Medicine." It showed that the mortality rate due to cardiac diseases was 50% lower among people who consumed 1 oz (30 g) of fish per day.

It was later proven that these two fatty acids (EPA and DHA) produced three types of prostaglandins which diminish platelet aggregation. This phenomenon increases blood fluidity which reduces the risks of thrombosis. Furthermore, EPA and DHA lower blood pressure and act as vasodilators. They are also responsible for reducing LDL-cholesterol, triglyceride levels and, to a lesser degree, HDL-cholesterol level.

It is therefore clear that since fish fats lower the cholesterol level and reduce the risks of cardiovascular diseases, the fattier the fish, the better it is for the well-being of the body! Consumption of salmon, tuna, sardines, mackerel, anchovies and herring should thus be strongly encouraged.

NOTE: It is equally important to know that the fat content of fish varies widely depending on the season and the fishing location. Fish fat levels can vary from one percent to 64 percent. Mackerel contains 32% fat before spawning and 18% after. The amount for sardines varies from one percent to thirty-two percent.

d) Monounsaturated fatty acids

Oleic acid is the main monounsaturated fatty acid. It can be found in olive oil. It helps reduce the "bad cholesterol" (LDL-cholesterol) level and increases the "good cholesterol" (HDL-cholesterol) level, which is what is desired.

Therefore, it is highly recommended for use in olive oil salad dressings and in cooking. Many will be happy to learn that tuna fish seasoned with olive oil is truly a weapon against cholesterol.

If the LDL-cholesterol level decreases by 11% and the HDL-cholesterol level increases by 11%, the rate of myocardial infarction and coronary ischemia decreases by 35%!

4) **Dietary fiber should be increased**

The presence of fibers in the gastrointestinal (GI) tract improves fat metabolism.

a) Pectin

Three apples added to the daily diet (i.e. .28 oz or 18 g of fibers and .07 oz or 2 g of pectin) over a two month period will decrease the cholesterol level by approximately five percent. This reduction is significant in patients whose cholesterol level is higher than 6.20 mmol/l. The HDL-cholesterol level over this period of time decreases by 20% and LDL-cholesterol by 80%. The apolipoprotein B level decreases by 6.4% and the apolipoprotein A1 level decreases by 1%, resulting in an improvement in the ApoB/ApoA1 atherogenic ratio. Despite the consumption of 2.8 oz or 80 g of assimilable carbohydrates per day, the glycemic level decreases by 7% to 13%, thereby favoring triglyceride reduction.

b) Carob

In normal subjects, carob lowers the total cholesterol level by 11% and the LDL-cholesterol level by 10%. Among hypercholesterolemic cases, the total cholesterol level decreases by 17% and the LDL-cholesterol level by 19%.

c) Guar gum

–guar gum pasta: the Italians make a type of pasta with two types of flour: hard wheat and guar-gum. By consuming 3.5 oz (100 g) of this pasta with 2.8 oz (80 g) of parmesan cheese and 1.75 oz (50 g) of butter added, the total cholesterol level decreases by 10%. The result might have been even better if no parmesan cheese were ingested and if butter were replaced by vegetable margarine.

–guar gum flour: Tagliafero's experiment proved that 0.14 oz (4 g) of this flour added to the diet four times a day leads to a decrease in the LDL-cholesterol level and an increase in the HDL-cholesterol level.

In mmol/l	Control	Guar-gum	Standard Deviation
Total cholesterol	4.40 ± 1.10	4.40 ± 1.00	p 0.05
Apolipoprotein A1	$2.30 \pm .50$	$2.90 \pm .80$	p 0.01
LDL-cholesterol	$3.20 \pm .90$	$2.80 \pm .70$	p 0.01

d) Bran has no effect on cholesterol metabolism. It even tends to decrease the effect of pectin if the two are taken together.

5) Increase the intake of vitamins A and E, selenium and chromium

a) Vitamin E

LDL oxidation plays an important role in accumulation of cellular cholesterol. Vitamin E protects the LDL from oxidation and reduces its uptake by cellular macrophages by more than 20%.

Vitamin E is found in grain, in vegetable oils, and, in smaller quantities, in butter, green vegetables, eggs and liver.

b) Vitamin A

The anti-oxidizing action of vitamin E is reinforced by vitamin A, found mostly in fish, mammal livers, dairy products and egg yolk.

A provitamin A (or carotenoid) is found in vegetables (carrots, spinach, cabbage, oranges, apricots) and is transformed into vitamin A in the intestinal cells.

c) Selenium

This mineral reinforces the action of the vitamin E by acting on glutathoine peroxidase to prevent the formation of free radicals and against excessive platelet aggregation. It is found in eggs, tuna, liver, red meat, garlic, beer yeast, wheat germ and whole grains.

d) Chromium

This mineral participates in the "glucose tolerance factor" which slows down lipogenesis. It reduces synthesis of LDL-cholesterol and increases the formation of HDL-cholesterol.

It is found in large quantities in liver, kidneys, cheese, whole grains, beer yeast and black pepper.

6) Limit coffee consumption

Studies by Framingham, in the United States, and by Tromso, in Norway, have shown that when more than six cups of coffee are consumed daily, the total cholesterol level clearly increases and the HDL-cholesterol level decreases slightly. Although the exact cause for this effect is not known, it is certain that caffeine is not the cause of this negative effect. Decaffeinated coffee has the same effect.

7) A little wine is all right

Whereas distilled alcohols (whisky, for example) should be avoided, Dr. Masquelier has shown that the tannin in wine contains procyanidine, a substance that causes the cholesterol level to decrease.

Some observers have even noted an increase in HDL-cholesterol levels due to this substance, but it seems that only the HDL 3 components increases. The anti-atherogenic component is HDL 2.

Crete, where a large quantity of wine and olive oil are consumed, has the lowest rate of cardiovascular disease in Europe!

F) IMPROVE YOUR LIFESTYLE

1) Stress

In individuals under stress, there is an augmentation in the catecholamine level. This increase favors synthesis of the LDL-cholesterol precursors and decreases the HDL-cholesterol level. Exactly how and why this occurs has yet to be determined. Without knowing the precise reason for this phenomenon, we do know that an effective stress management or relaxation method is the key to avoiding such ill effects.

2) Smoking

Tobacco causes a decrease in the HDL-cholesterol level. It is important to stop smoking.

3) A sedentary lifestyle

A lack of physical activity is harmful. Exercise helps reduce the triglyceride level and increase the HDL-cholesterol level, particularly the HDL 2 fraction which is the most anti-atherogenic.

To obtain statistically significant results against cholesterol, it is important to practice a physical activity for at least twenty minutes three times a week. The best type of exercise is an endurance sport. Yet jogging six miles a week results in only a small decrease in the cholesterol level. In order to receive a sharp decrease in the total cholesterol level and an increase in the HDL-cholesterol level, it is necessary to run 36 miles a week; this is the minimum for a serious long-distance runner!

G) IN SUM, TO DECREASE YOUR CHOLESTEROL LEVEL, YOU MUST:

–lose weight if you are obese
–cut down on meat consumption (5 oz/day maximum)
–eat lean meats (lean beef)
–substitute poultry (without skin) for meat whenever possible
–avoid cold cuts and organ meats
–increase fish consumption (10 oz per week minimum)
–eat little or no butter (.35 oz per day maximum)
–limit cheese consumption
–drink skim milk and eat non-fat dairy products
–increase fiber consumption (fruits, cereals, vegetables)
–increase vegetable mono and polyunsaturated fatty acid consumption (olive, sunflower and rapeseed oil)
–make sure selenium, chromium, vitamin A & E intake is sufficient
–do not drink too much coffee
–if you feel the need, drink wine that is rich in tannin (1/2 bottle/day maximum)
–control stress level
–practice an endurance sport if you can
–quit smoking

BIBLIOGRAPHY

SPECIFICS ON CHOLESTEROL

BASDEVANT A., TRAYNARD P.Y.   *Hypercholestérolémie Symptômes* 1988 n° 12

BRUCKERT E.   *Les dyslipidémies Impact Médecin*; Dossier du Practicien n° 20, 1989

LUC G., DOUSTE-BLAZY P., FRUCHART J.C   *Le cholestérol, d'où vient-il? Comment circule-t-il? Où va-t-il?* Rev. Prat. 1989, 39, 12, 1011–1017

POLONOWSKI J.   *Régulation de l'absorption intestinale du cholestérol* Cahiers Nutr. Diet. 1989, 1, 19-25

FATS AND CHOLESTEROL

Consensus — *Conference on lowering blood cholesterol to prevent heart disease* JAMA 1985, 253, 2080–2090

BETTERIDGE D.J. — *High Density lipoprotein and coronary heart disease* Brit. Med. J. 15 Avril 1989, 974–975

DURAND G. *and al.* — *Effets comparés d'huiles végétales et d'huiles de poisson sur le cholestérol du rat.* Med et Nutr. 1985, XXI, N° 6, 391–406

DYERBERG J. *and al.* — *Eicosapentaenoic acid and prevention of thrombosis and atherosclerosis?* Lancet 1978, 2, 117–119

ERNST E., LE MIGNON D. — *Les acides gras omega 3 et l'artériosclérose* CR de Ther. 1987, V, N° 56, 22–25

FIELD C. — *The influence of eggs upon plasma cholesterol levels* Nutr. Rev. 1983, 41. N° 9, 242–244

FOSSATI P., FERMONC. — *Huiles de poisson, intérêt nutritionnel et prévention de l'athéromatose* N.P.N. Med. 1988, VIII, 1–7

DE GENNES J.L., TURPING TRFFERT J. — *Correction thérapeutique des hyperlipidémies idiopathiques héréditaires. Bilan d'une consultation diététique standardisée* Nouv. Presse Med. 1973, 2, 2457–2464

GRUNDY M.A. — *Comparison of monosaturated fatty acids and carbohydrates for lowering plasma cholesterol* N. Engl. J. Med. 1986, 314, 745–749

HAY, C.R.M. — *Effect of fish oil on platelet kinetics in patients with ischaemic heart disease* The Lancet 5 Juin 1982, 1269–1272

KRMHOUT D., BOSSCHIETER E.B., LEZENNE-COULANDER C. — *The inverse relation between fish consumption and 20 year mortality from coronary heart disease* New Engl. J. Med. 1985, 312, 1205–1209

LEAF A., WEBER P.C. — *Cardiovascular effects of n-3 fatty acids* New Engl. J. Med. 1988, 318, 549–557

LEMARCHAL P. — *Les acides gras polyinsaturés en Omega 3* Cah. Nutr. Diet. 1985, XX, 2, 97–102

MARINER E. — *Place des acides gras polyinsaturés de la famille n-3 dans le traitement des dyslipoprotéinémies* Med. Dig. Nutr. 1986, 53, 14–16

MARWICK C. — *What to do about dietary satured fats?* JAMA 1989, 262, 453

PHILLIPSON and al. — *Reduction of plasma lipids, lipoproteins and apoproteins by dietary fish oils in patients with hypertriglyceridemia* New Engl. J. Med. 1985, 312, 1210–1216

PICLET G. — *Le poisson, aliment, composition, intéret nutritionnel* Cah. Nutr. Diet. 1987, XXII, 317–336

THORNGREN M. — *Effects of 11 week increase in dietary eicosapentaenoïc acid on bleeding time, lipids and platelet aggregation* Lancet 28 Nov. 1981, 1190–11

TURPIN G. — *Régimes et médicaments abaissant la cholestérolémie* Rev. du Prat. 1989, 39, 12, 1024–1029

VLES R.O. — *Les acides gras essentiels en physiologie cardio-vasculaire* Ann. Nutr. Alim. 1980, 34, 255–264

WOODCOCK B.E. — *Beneficial effect of fish oil on blood viscosity in peripheral vascular disease* Br. Med. J. Vol. 288 du 25 février 1984, p. 592–594

ALIMENTARY FIBERS AND HYPERCHOLESTEROLEMIA

ANDERSON J.W.　*Dietary fiber, lipids and atherosclerosis* Am. J. Cardiol. 1987, 60, 17–22

GIRAULT A.　*Effets bénéfiques de la consommation de pommes sur le métabolisme lipidique chez l'homme.* Entretiens de Bichat 28 Septembre 1988

LEMONNIER D.,
DOUCHE C.,
FLAMENT C.　*Effet du son et de la pectine sur les lipides sériques du rat* Cah. Nutr. Diet. 1983, XVIII, 2, 99

RAUTUREAU J.,
COSTE T.,　*Effets des fibres alimentaires sur le métabolisme du cholestérol* Cah. Nutr. Diet. 1983, XVIII, 2, 84–88

KARSENTI P.
SABLE-AMPLIS R.,
SICART R., BARON A.　*Influence des fibres de pomme sur les taux d'esters de cholestérol du foi, de l'intestin et de l'aorte* Cah. Nutr. Diet. 1983, XVII, 297

TAGLIAFFERRO V. and al.　*Moderate guar-gum addition to usual diet improves peripheral sensibility to insulin and lipaemic profile in NIDDM* Diabète et Métabolisme 1985, 11, 380–385

TOGNARELLI M.　*Guar-pasta: a new diet for obese subjects B* Acta Diabet. Lat. 1986, 23, 77

TROWELL H.　*Dietary fiber and coronary heart disease* Europ. J. Clin. Biol. Res. 1972, 17, 345

VAHOUNY G.U.　*Dietary fiber, lipid metabolism and atherosclerosis* Fed. Proc. 1982, 41, 2801–2806

ZAVOLAL J.H.　*Effets hypolipéniques d'aliments contenant du caroube* Am. J. Clin. Nutr. 1983, 38, 285–294

VITAMINS, TRACE ELEMENTS AND HYPERCHOLESTEROLEMIA

1) Vitamin E

CAREW T.E.　*Antiatherogenic effect of probucol unrelated to its hypocholesterolemic effect P.N.A.S.* USA June 1984, Vol. 84 p. 7725–7729

FRUCHART J.C.　*Influence de la qualité des LD sur leur métabolisme et leur athérogénicité (inédit)*

JURGENS G.　*Modifications of human serum LDL by oxydation* Chemistry and Physics of lipids 1987, 45, 315–336

STREINBRECHER V.P.　*Modifications of LDL by endothelial cells involves lipid peroxydation P.N.A.S.* USA June 1984, Vol. 81, 3883–3887

2) Selenium

LUOMA P.V.　*Serum selenium, gluthathione peroxydase, lipids, and human liver microsomal enzyme activity* Biological Trace Element Research 1985, 8, 2, 113–121

MITCHINSON M.J.　*Possible role of deficiency of selenium and vitamin E in atherosclerosis* J. Clin. Pathol. 1984, 37, 7, 837

SALONEN J.T.　*Serum fatty acids, apolipoproteins, selenium and vitamin antioxydants and risk of death from coronary artery disease* Am. J. Cardiol. 1985, 56, 4, 226–231

3) Chromium

ABRAHAM A.S.　*The effect of chromiuon established atherosclerotic plaques in rabbits* Am. J. Clin. Nutr. 1980, 33, 2294–2298

GORDON T.   *High density lipoprotein as a protective factor against coronary heart disease* The Framingham study Am. J. Med. 1977, 62, 707

OFFENBACHER E.G.   *Effect of chromium-rich yeast on glucose tolerance a blood lipids in elderly subjects* Diabetes 1980, 29, 919–925

COFFEE AND HYPERCHOLESTEROLEMIA

ARNESEN E.   *Coffee and serum cholesterol* Br. Med. J. 1984, 288, 1960

HERBERT P.N.   *Caffeine does not affect lipoprotein metabolism* Clin. res. 1987, 35, 578A

HILL C.   *Coffee consumption and cholesterol concentration* Letter to editor Br. Med. J. 1985, 920, 1590

THELLE D.S.   *Coffee and cholesterol in epidemiological and experimental studies* Atherosclerosis 1987, 67, 97–103

THELLE D.S.   *The Tromso Heart Study. Does coffee raise serum cholesterol?* N. Engl. J. Med. 1983, 308, 1454–1457

IDEAL WEIGHT

When we measure ourselves, what exactly are we measuring? Usually, it is the total body weight, including bones, muscle, fat, organs, viscera, nerves and water. Fat makes up 15% of the total body mass in men and 22% in women.

Obesity is defined as excess body fat, surpassing average weight by at least 20%. We associate obesity with excess weight, even if the scale does not reveal the exact ratio of fat mass to active mass (e.g. muscles, organs). How can we measure the exact amount of fat in the body?

One way is to measure a fold of skin with a compass, but this is not a reliable method. Instead of using the weight charts strictly established by insurance companies, or the skin fold method, it is better to use the Lorenz formula (height in cm and weight in kg) in order to understand the concept of ideal weight:

Weight (men)   = (Height − 100) − 1/4 (Height − 150)

Weight (women) = (Height − 100) − 1/2 (Height − 150)

This formula does not, however, take into account age or the skeletal structure.

The Quetelet index or BMI (Body Mass Index) – weight/height (2) – is commonly used nowadays to define the relationship between weight and height squared.

BMI = Weight (kg)/Height$(^2)$ (m^2)

The average BMI for men is 20–25. For women it is 19–24. Any higher value, up to 30, signifies excess weight. If the value is higher than 30, the subject is considered obese. If the BMI is higher than 40, the case is medically alarming.

This definition is medical and not aesthetic but the BMI concept is useful because it is linked to the notion of fat-mass

The way fat is distributed determines the prognosis for obesity. This distribution is measured using the following ratio.

$$\frac{\text{waist measurement (at the navel)}}{\text{hip measurement (at fullest part)}}$$

It is generally 0.85 for men and 0.65 to 0.85 for women.

In android obesity, most is accumulated in the upper body (face, neck, abdomen above the navel). The ratio is always greater than 1.

Complications arrive early and are frequent: diabetes, hypercholesterolemia, high blood pressure, cardiovascular risks.

In gynecoid obesity, the fat mass is found essentially in the lower body (hips, buttocks, thighs, lower belly). This distribution is normal in the female body. The risks of complications are lower. The problem exists more from an aesthetic point of view than anything. The worst aspect of the problem is that this type of obesity may result in cellulitis.

Beyond the medical statistics, which try to describe scientifically what is more an aesthetic concern or a discomfort, the most important weight value is one at which the patient will feel the most comfortable. In sum, the goal should be a weight that gives the patient a sense of well-being.

This weight may sometimes be greater than the weight calculated by theoretical standards, but we really should not be concerned about this. If an obese person can reach this weight, then it is a more realistic goal than theoretical ideals established by doctors, which may even cause discouragement if the goal is too severe.

On the other hand, women are often overly influenced by media images. They should realize that a fantastic and unrealistic weight goal has no justification. Their bodies, fully equipped with reasonable regulatory systems, will prevent them from reaching such a goal.

The ideal – if it exists – should be carefully thought out by the obese person and if necessary, with the critical help of a doctor.

THE CALORIE THEORY

When food is placed in a calorimeter, the energy it contains can be calculated. For example: 3.5 oz of honey releases 290 calories, 3.5 oz of butter 750 calories, 3.5 oz of codfish 80 calories, and 3.5 oz pork 380 calories.

– .035 oz of protein release 4 calories
– .035 oz of carbohydrate release 4 calories
– .035 oz of fat release 9 calories
– .035 oz of alcohol release 7 calories

The term concept of "calories" is often misused. The word "calories" is actually a simplified version of the term kilocalories. And, if we really wanted to respect the international terms, we would count in kilojoules, where one kilocalorie is equal to 4.18 kilojoules.

The human body, to put it very simply, has too often been compared to a boiler: if intake is greater than the body's expenditures and not everything is "burned", the excess calories accumulate, and the subject gains weight. If, on the other hand, the calorie ration is inferior to the daily calorie requirement, the organism must, theoretically, draw upon its fat reserves and the subject should lose weight.

This reasoning ignores the human body's ability to regulate and adopt itself and denies the individual particularities that make each person unique!

Contrary to popular belief, an obese person is not necessarily someone who eats too much. In an obese population:

– only 15% over-eat (2,800 – 4,000 cal/day)
– 35% eat normally (2,000 – 2,700 cal/day)
– 50% eat little (less than 2,000 cal/day)

World class athletes are able to maintain a stable weight with caloric inputs ranging from 2,500 to 12,000 calories per day, according to the individual and the sport. The marathon runner, Alain Mimoun, maintained his weight and underwent difficult training on only 2,000 calories per day, whereas the cyclist, Jacques Anquetil, needed 6,000 calories to balance his diet and maintain a stable weight.

The differences in caloric intake are minimal among slim, normal, fat and obese individuals, as is proven by the studies of Doctors Bellisle and Roland-Cachera, who divided the studied subjects into five categories using the B.M.I. Index (Weight/Height^2).

By examining the following graphs, it becomes evident that there is no correlation between daily calorie rations and corpulence. Obese and fat people do not automatically eat any more than slim and thin ones.

However, by classifying children according to their father's profession, it appears that among children with similar BMI indices, those whose fathers are blue collar workers eat more than those whose fathers are office workers or executives

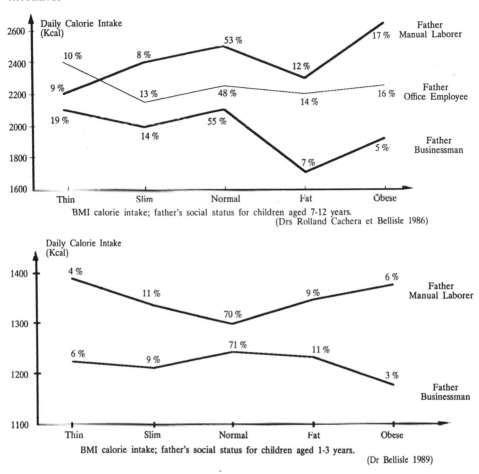

BMI calorie intake; father's social status for children aged 7-12 years.
(Drs Rolland Cachera et Bellisle 1986)

BMI calorie intake; father's social status for children aged 1-3 years.
(Dr Bellisle 1989)

Yet this data does not prevent most weight loss methods from being based upon a hypocaloric approach. The reasoning goes like this:

If the necessary daily ration for an adult is 2,500 calories and he is given a 2,000 calorie diet, a 500 calorie deficit results. His body is then forced to supplement the diet by drawing the missing 500 calories from the fat reserves, and the individual loses weight.

But, what actually occurs is the following: when the body is faced with this input deficit, it eventually adjusts the offer to the demand. That is to say, if it is given no more than 2,000 calories, it will function on only 2,000 calories.

Consequently, there is no longer an energy deficit. The fat reserves are no

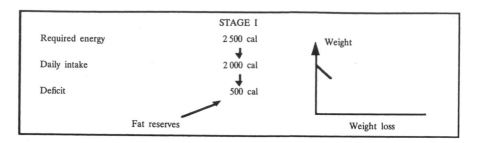

longer required and the weight stabilizes. The subject may believe that he has reached a plateau in his weight-loss and waits confidently.

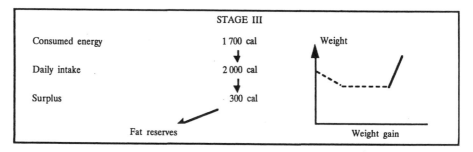

In this stage, the body "remembers" its previous frustrations. What if its daily ration were to be reduced again? Triggered by its survival instinct, the body decides to spend no more than 1,700 calories in order to save 300 calories in case new rationing happens. The 300 calorie surplus is stored away and the subject gains even more weight.

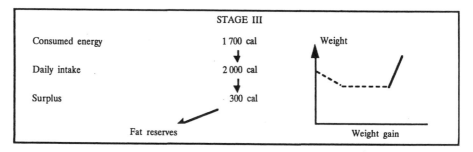

Worried by his new weight gain, the subject visits his doctor or nutritionist, who doubts the patient's story. The patient is suspected of having miscalculated his caloric intake or of having secretly binged on the side. In sum, the obese subject is assumed to be incapable of following directions, or even worse, a liar! To ensure the results, the doctor lowers the daily caloric ration and gives new

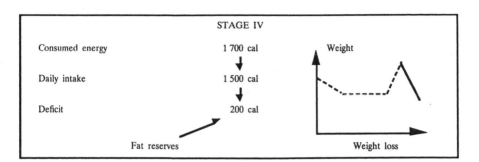

advice, and the subject leaves with a 1,500 calorie diet as well as renewed hopes.

A few weeks later, we find that the patient's body, having functioned on 1,700 calories, is again taken by surprise, and further weight-loss occurs.

As we have seen already, the body is on guard for a decreased caloric intake. Subsequently, the regulatory system is triggered more quickly, and the weight-loss phase is shorter and not as noticeable. A new plateau has now been reached

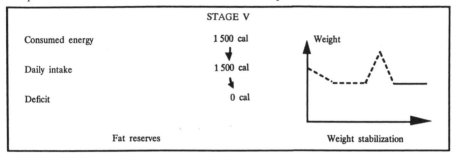

because the organism has readjusted to the imposed rationing.

By this time, we know that the body's ancestral survival instinct has worked to build up reserves while consuming no more than 1,200 calories daily. Once again, the patient starts to gain weight.

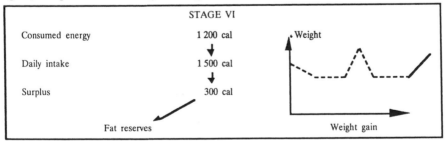

At this point, the patient now understands that weight-loss occurs if the food ration is continuously diminished. Using calorie tables, he calculates a 1,000 calorie diet for himself.

An emphemeral weight-loss phase follows once again, but is quickly halted when weight stabilization is attained. Weight gain occurs and the subject now exceeds his initial weight. The organism was on its guard and it quickly triggered its protective system. At the slightest calorie intake, it stored a maximum of surplus food.

Those accustomed to hypocaloric diets can bear witness that the slightest dietary mistake, "because it's the weekend", can make them gain four to five pounds within one or two days.

The obese patient thus watches his weight like bouncing a rubber ball. At the slightest lack of discipline, it goes bounding up.

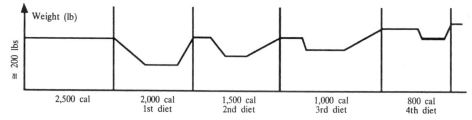

Finally, the more the subject rations himself, the more his body tends to create reserves. Some individuals who weighed 154 lbs. for example, and who only had 10 lbs. to lose, found themselves weighing 158 lbs. at the end of the diet.

In the hypocaloric diet, the calorie ration must be continuously reduced in order for weight-loss to occur. But in the end, the less one eats, the more one gains weight!

Doctors are therefore confronted with a clientele, who, at the price of a severely controlled diet and enormous frustrations, manage to gain weight (or do not lose any) on an 800 calorie diet – not to mention the fact that the reduced intake leads to fatigue, low blood pressure and even depression. In addition, the patient risks becoming anorexic at any time. At this point, all they need to do is switch doctors, going from a nutritionalist to a psychiatrist!

Yet the sawtooth pattern of such diets that cause successive weight gain and weight-loss is well known, and has even been demonstrated in animals.

Professor Bronwell, of the University of Pennsylvania, studied this phenomenon on a population of rats alternated between high and low calorie diets: over the course of the first diet, the rats lost weight in 21 days and gained back the weight over a period of 46 days. Over the course of the second diet, the rats lost the same amount of weight over a 46 day period and regained everything in 14 days!

Later weight-loss is more difficult to achieve, and weight gain is more and more rapid. It has therefore been proven that the metabolism adapts itself to calorie reductions. Every caloric deficit can lower the metabolic expenditures by 50%, but every return to the norm, however brief, is accompanied by weight gain. The greater the difference between the diet and normal intake the quicker weight regain occurs.

Suffice it to say that it is not enough to follow a 1,500 calorie diet if the calories consumed are unbalanced. For example, a person who consumes a coke and a bologna sandwich on white bread has obviously missed the point. The diet must also include a proper balance of carbohydrates, fibers and minerals in order to have a positive effect on weight-loss.

BIBLIOGRAPHY

ASTIER-DUMAS M.
Densité calorique, densité nutritionnelle, repères pour le choix des aliments Med. Nutr. 1984, XX, 4, 229–234

BELLISLE F.
Obesity and food intake in children: evidence for a role of metabolic and/or behavioral daily rhythms Appetite 1988, 11, 111–118

BROWNELL K.D.
The effects of repeated cycles of weight-loss and regain in rats Phys. Behavior 1986, 38, 459–464

HERAUD G.
Densité nutritionnelle des aliments Gaz. Med. FR. 1988, 95, 13, 39–42

LEIBEL R.J.
Diminished energy requirements in reduced obese persons Metabolism 1984, 33, 164–170

LOUIS-SYLVESTRE J.
Poids accordéon: de plus en plus difficile à perdre Le Gén. 1989, 1087, 18–20

ROLLAND-CACHERA M.F., BELLISLEF
No correlation between adiposity and food intake: why are working class children fatter? Am. J. Clin. Nutr. 1986, 44, 779–787

ROLAND-CACHERA M.F., DEHEEGER M.
Adiposity and food intake in young children: the environmental challenge to individual susceptibility Br. Med. J. 1988, 296, 1037–1038

RUASSE J.P.
Des calories, pourquoi? Combien? Coll. L'indispensable en Nutrition 1987

SPITZER L., RODIN J.
Human eating behavior: a critical review of study in normal weight and overweight individuals Appetite 1981, 2, 293

URASSE J.P.
L'approche homéopathique du traitement des obésités Paris 1988

INSULIN

A) INTRODUCTION

Insulin is a polypeptidic hormone secreted by the islets of Langherans in the pancreas. It is the endocrine secretion of the pancreas. It maintains glycemia at around 5.5 mmol/l.

From a physiological point of view, it is the only substance responsible for glycoregulation in normal subjects. Catecholamines and glucagon only play this role in exceptional circumstances.

B) INSULIN SECRETION

There is a weak and continual basal secretion of insulin (2 to 20 microU/ml) which controls the secretion of hepatic glucose when the subject is in a fasting state or between meals. However, it is too weak to cause lipogenesis, i.e. the accumulation of fat reserves.

At the beginning of a meal there is a phase of insulin production in the head of the pancreas resulting in an instantaneous small secretion peak of low intensity, lasting only a few minutes. It is triggered by the mere sight of food or contact of the tongue's anterior taste buds with any substance. This response can be considered as a preparation for a meal.

The peak is rapidly followed by a drop which is then followed by a second peak in the post-prandial phase. Insulin secretion therefore depends on the extent of the glycemic increase. It favors intracellular penetration of glucose and its storage in the form of glycogen and triglycerides. This anabolising process, lipogenesis, occurs only when there are large amounts of circulating insulin.

C) REGULATING INSULIN SECRETION

1) **Glucose** is the substrate that stimulates the B-cells of the pancreas. But other carbohydrates have the same effect: galactose, fructose, mannose, ribose, xylitol and ribitol. Xylose and arabinose, on the other hand, have no such impact.

2) **Lipids:** certain intermediaries in fat metabolism such as ketonic substrates, butyrate, propionate and octanoate may favor insulin secretion. This has been proven in *in vitro* experiments but the concentrations found *in vivo* are physiologically insignificant.

Malaisse proved that a diet based on fats causes the plasmatic insulin level to decrease; but in order to avoid an atherogenic effect, it is necessary to limit the intake of saturated fats and instead favor consumption of mono and polyun-saturated fats.

3) **Protein:** amino acids, particularly leucine and arginine, can increase insulin secretion. But again, this phenomenon occurs at plasmatic concentrations that are never found in physiological conditions.

4) **Other factors favoring insulin secretion:**

- glucagon
- glucocorticoid
- cyclic AMP
- intestinal hormones (secretin, gastrin, entero-glucagon)
- estrogen
- thyroxin
- growth hormone
- stimulation of the Vagus nerve (X)
- stimulation of the B-receptors and inhibition of the alpha-receptors
- calcium, magnesium and potassium ions
- caffeine
  theophylline
  sulfonylureas

5) **Factors inhibiting insulin secretion**

- fasting state
- weight-loss
- hypoxia
- insulin
- glucosamine
- catecholamines (epinephrine, norepinephrine)
- inhibition of the Vagus nerve
- stimulation of the alpha-receptors and betablocking agents
- alloxan
- streptozotocine
- diazoxide
- phenethylbiguanide
- diuretic substances

D) HOW INSULIN WORKS

1) **On water metabolism:** favors water retention by causing sodium retention.

2) **On protein metabolism:** favors the intracellular penetration of amino acids.

3) **On carbohydrate metabolism:** triggers a drop in glycemia as a result of cellular absorption of glucose.

4) **On fat metabolism:** favors lipogenesis and consequently, the formation of fat reserves:

- by causing excess glucose to be transformed into fatty acids,
- by stimulating the lipoprotein lipase which allows circulating fatty acids to be stored as fat reserves in the form of triglycerides,
- by increasing the volume of fat cells,
- by inhibiting triglyceride lipase, which normally would be responsible for lipolysis,
- and by neutralizing the lipolytic effect of cortisol and the catecholamines.

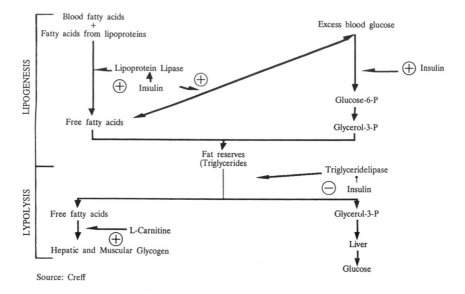

Source: Creff

In the cases of hyperinsulinism, the whole metabolism is geared toward lipogenesis. The fat reserves subsequently increase, and therefore, so does weight. This phenomenon is reinforced since lipolysis is impossible, as insulin inhibits the action of triglyceride lipase, which would normally cause the breakdown of fat reserves.

With the Montignac method, when we avoid carbohydrates with a high glycemic index, we eliminate hyperglycemic peaks. Consequently, insulin secretion decreases progressively. Once the insulin level is low enough (often less than 20 mU/ml), the lipogenesis system becomes physiologically impossible and it is "turned off" and lipolysis is "turned on." Hence, in the long term, weight-loss puts an end to insulin resistance. The phenomenon is, however, always reversible; this is what eventually ensures weight stability.

E) INSULIN AND OBESITY

Eating too many carbohydrates with a high glycemic index results in hyperglycemic peaks which induce high insulin secretion. At first, hyperinsulinism corrects hyperglycemia in the post-prandial phase. Then there is a decrease in glucose tolerance and glucose is inefficiently used peripherally. It takes a long time to penetrate the adipose, muscular and hepatic tissues. This is the insulin resistance stage: the insulin receptors are not as numerous, abnormalities in the post-receptors occur and the tyrosine kinase properties of the insulin receptors are altered.

As a result, in the second stage, the insulin is not correctly recognized by the gluco-dependent tissues which are not properly informed of the presence of insulin. Since the sugar is slow to enter the tissues, the glycemic level remains high for too long and a second secretion of insulin occurs. This simply aggravates the hyperinsulinism.

In the third stage, insulin resistance affects the pancreas; there is a slow-down in the normal drop in insulin secretion, which further aggravates hyperinsulinism.

The question is whether or not hyperinsulinism and insulin resistance are a primitive abnormality or a consequence of obesity.

Clark studied both these hypotheses:

The Case of Primitive Abnormality:

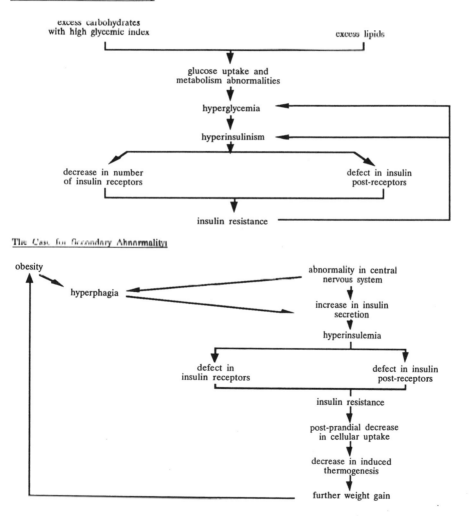

209

Hyperinsulinism most definitely plays an important role in obesity and insulin resistance. However, a secondary factor may be involved: the brown adipose tissue, specialized in heat generation, presents a number of abnormalities in obese persons. There is a decrease in thermogenesis which is normally induced by cold and by food consumption. This explains how weight increase is possible without hyperphagia.

F) THE MORBID DANGERS OF HYPERINSULINISM

It was long believed that hyperglycemia was more dangerous than hyperinsulinism. But, in fact, it is hyperinsulinism that increases the risk of arteriosclerosis with vascular, and specifically coronary incidents.

Hyperinsulinism is related to android obesity, periodic high blood pressure, hypertriglyceridemia, a decrease in the HDL-cholesterol level, hyperuricemia, excessive platelet hyperaggregation and sodium retention.

Moreover, hyperinsulinism plays a role in the alteration of the arterial walls because it facilitates the proliferation of smooth muscle cells and increases the LDL bonds to these cells.

Hyperinsulinism occurs when the blood insulin level is higher than 20mU/ml on an empty stomach or higher than 80mU/ml in the post-prandial phase.

BIBLIOGRAPHY

BASDEVANT A.   *Influence de la distribution de la masse sur le risque vasculaire* La Presse Médicale 1987, 16, 4

CLARK M.G.   *Obesity with insulin resistance. Experimental insights* Lancet, 1983, 2, 1236–1240

FROMAN L.A.   *Effect of vagotomy and vagal stimulation on insulin secretion* Diabetes 1967, 16, 443–448

GROSS P.   *De l'obésité au diabète* L'actualité diabétologique N° 13, p. 1–9

GUY-GRAND B.   *Variation des acides gras libres plasmatiques au cours des hyperglycémies provoquées par voie orale* Journées de Diabétologie de l'Hôtel-Dieu 1968, p. 319

GUY-GRAND B.   *Rôle éventuel du tissu adipeux dans l'insulino-résistance* Journées de Diabétologie de l'Hôtel-Dieu 1972, 81–92

JEANRENAUD B.   *Dysfonctionnement du système nerveux. Obésité et résistance à l'insuline* M/S Médecine-Sciences 1987, 3, 403–410

JEANRENAUD B.   *Insulin and obesity* Diabetologia, 1979, 17, 135–138

KOLTERMAN O.G.

Mechanisms of insulin resistance in human obesity. Evidence for receptor and post-receptor effects J. Clin. Invest. 1980, 65, 1272–1284

LAMBERT A.E.

Enhancement by caffeine of glucagon-induced and tolbutamide-induced insulin release from isolated foetal pancreatic tissue Lancet, 1967, 8, 819–820

LAMBERT A.E.

Organocultures de pancréas foetal de rat: étude morphologique et libération d'insuline in vitro Journées de Diabètologie de l'Hôtel-Dieu 1969, 115–129

LARSON B.

Abdominal adipose tissue distribution, obesity and risk of cardiovascular disease and death Br. Med. J. 1984, 288, 1402–1404

LE MARCHAND-BRUSTEL Y.

Résistance à l'insuline dans l'obésité M/S Médecine-Sciences 1987, 3, 394–402

LINQUETTE C.

Précis d'endocrinologie Ed. Masson 1973, p. 658–666

LOUIS-SYLVESTRE J.

La phase céphalique de sécrétion d'insuline Diabète et métabolisme 1987, 13, 63–73

MARKS V.

Action de différents stimuli sur l'insulinosécrétion humaine: influence du tractus gastro-intestinal Journées de Diabétologie de l'Hôtel-Dieu 1969, 179–190

MARLISSE E.B.

Système nerveux central et glycorégulation Journées de Diabétologie de l'Hôtel-Dieu 1975, 7–21

MEYLAN M.

Metabolic factors in insulin resistance in human obesity Metabolism 1987, 36, 256–261

WOODS S.C.

Interaction entre l'insulinosécrétion et le système nerveux central Journées de Diabétologie de l'Hôtel-Dieu 1983

FUNCTIONAL HYPOGLYCEMIA

A) PHYSIOPATHOLOGY

In the morning on an empty stomach, the glycemic level is approximately 5.5 mmol/l. If the subject eats a balanced breakfast, the glycemic rate will increase to 7.7 mmol/l and, in response to the insulin's action, will drop to 5.5 mmol/l after two hours, and continue to decrease to 3.85 mmol/l during the third hour, before it again reverts to 5.5 mmol/l (see graph I).

However, if the subject consumes an excessive amount of carbohydrates with a high glycemic index (white bread, honey, jam, sugared coffee or tea, commercial fruit juices rich in saccharose) or drinks alcohol mixed with a sweet drink on an empty stomach, the result is a high glycemic peak after 20 minutes. At this point, the pancreas endocrine intervenes, reducing the glycemic rate, but the drop is often significant and can reach 2.48 mmol/l causing hypoglycemia (see graph II).

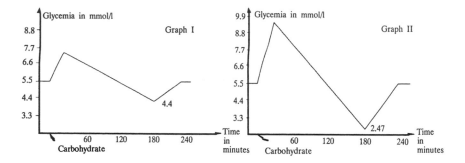

If the glycemic level drops drastically, the subject will experience a number of symptoms. These symptoms include paleness, palpitations, perspiration, anxiety, shakes, sharp hunger pangs and other discomforts such as a loss of consciousness, which is the classic hypoglycemic symptom. Patients need to understand that if they are in a hypoglycemic state at 11:00 a.m., it is because they consumed an excessive amount of certain carbohydrates three hours earlier. Contrary to their belief that their condition is due to a lack of sugar, the real reason is that they have digested too many high-glycemia carbohydrates which then provoke severe hypoglycemia.

Usually, the glycemic level drops progressively, with more ordinary symptoms. This prevents the doctor from making an accurate diagnosis. Some of these symptoms are headaches, yawning, fatigue, irritability, aggressiveness, blurred vision, memory gaps, lack of concentration, dyslexia and chills. These symptoms are the patients' most common complaints and are often attributed to fatigue or to the beginnings of cerebral ischemia. They can, however, be signs of hypoglycemia. These signs then should not be overlooked or neglected. Functional cases of hypoglycemia are found in 19% of subjects of normal weight and in 31% of obese subjects.

It must be noted that some certain subjects may be victims of genuine hypoglycemia and yet do not show any symptoms. Others may complain of discomforts suggesting hypoglycemia which are not confirmed by blood sugar levels measured during the periods of malaise. Similarly, the glycemic level at which troubles appear varies: certain cases of hypoglycemia at 3.85 mmol/l are very badly tolerated whereas others are well tolerated at 2.47 mmol/l.

B) DIAGNOSIS

To confirm diagnosis of functional hypoglycemia, the clinical signs described above should be observed:

- the symptoms should appear when the subject has not eaten, a few hours after a meal or following physical exertion;
- they should disappear soon after consuming sugary foods.

It is important that hypoglycemia be biologically confirmed:

- orally provoked hyperglycemia is useful, but it can lead to false positive diagnoses;
- the tolerance test based on a standardized breakfast is more reliable;
- an increase of insulemia or plasmatic cortisol is an argument in favor of the diagnosis;
- but the ideal way to confirm it is to measure the glycemic level during periods of malaise by sampling a drop of blood from the finger and to dose the glucose level with a filleted automatic hand analyzer. In fact, the only conclusive sign is a glycemic level below 2.75 mmol/l during the discomfort.

C) ETIOLOGY

Can certain mechanisms cause post-prandial functional hypoglycemia?

1) *Hyperinsulinism and insulin resistance* are common in the obese subject and facilitate secondary hypoglycemia. Hyperinsulinism is increased by coffee or alcohol absorption.

2) *Unsynchronized insulin secretion*: A delay in insulin secretion in relation to the glycemic peak. It is a sign of glucose intolerance. In this case, the patient runs the risk of becoming diabetic.

3) In rare cases, *insulin secretion is deactivated by auto-antibodies*: The resulting hyperglycemia provokes further insulin secretion. Then, the antigen-antibody complex acts like a veritable "insulin delayer" which will act late after the meal and cause hypoglycemia.

4) Sometimes, insulin secretion is quantitatively normal, but *insulin hypersensitivity* develops.

5) The release of insulin can be potentialized by an excessive release of gastroenteric hormones: gastrin, entero-glucagon, gastric inhibitory peptides (GIP).

6) Insufficient *neoglycogenesis* can occur: upon awakening, the body produces 75% of its glucose comes from glycogen and 25% from neoglycogenesis. There are 5.40 oz (150 g) of glycogen in the muscles and 2.70 oz (75 g) of glycogen in the liver. There is considerably less circulating blood glucose, approximately

.70 oz (20 g). The body consumes about .25 oz (7 g) of glucose per hour. It therefore has sufficient reserves for twelve hours. Neoglycogenesis functions more or less regularly depending on the dietary intake. When it functions poorly, this can cause hypoglycemia.

7) These phenomena are often related to an excessive vagal tonicity. It causes an acceleration of gastric emptying, a factor of hyperinsulinism. It provoked gastric hyperacidity, which leads to hypersensitivity of the pancreatic Beta cells. This results in exaggerated insulin secretion out of proportion with the glycemic level.

This vagotomy which occurs is often encountered in anxious subjects who tend to somatize, as is the case with spasmophilia. Indeed, some symptoms of hypoglycemia are also typical signs of panic. This is why it is important to establish a psychological profile of patients suffering from functional hypoglycemia.

D) TREATMENT

- The goal is to reduce the post-prandial hyperglycemic peak in order to limit insulin secretion and avoid secondary hypoglycemia.
- Dietary precautions should focus on breakfast.
- As the Montignac method suggests, carbohydrates with a high glycemic index (white bread, jam, honey, saccharose, sodas) should be eliminated from the diet.

Breakfast should be a high-protein and high-fat (preferably polyunsaturated fatty acids) meal. If necessary, its fiber content should be increased (e.g. with fruits). This reduces the post-prandial glycemic peak.

Coffee should not be drunk in excessive amounts. Caffeine increases insulin secretion. Also, avoid drinking alcohol on an empty stomach, especially if it is mixed with a sweet beverage (e.g. whiskey & coke, gin & tonic, vodka & orange juice).

These precautions are often sufficient, but it is sometimes recommended to snack between meals at 11:00 a.m. and at 4:00 p.m. Obese subjects must lose enough weight to make insulin resistance disappear and to correct hyperinsulinism. If nervous troubles occur, psychotherapy, yoga or relaxation will correct neurovegetative dystonia.

It is important to remember that post-prandial functional hypoglycemia also affects non-diabetic subjects and may be aggravated by some common prescription medications: aspirin, oxytetracycline, haloperidol, manganese, beta-blocking agents and destropropoxyphen-paracetamol.

Part One

On the other hand, medication is rarely necessary to treat hypoglycemia. Some form of drug may eventually be prescribed if carefully followed hygieno-dietetic health and dietary measures fail: oral antidiabetics, calcium gluconate, anticholinergics, anxiolytics and gastric dumping modifiers.

BIBLIOGRAPHY

CAHILL G.F. — *A non-editorial on non-hypoglycemia* N. Engl. J. Med. 1974, 291, 905 906

CATHELINEAU G. — *Effect of calcium infusion on post-reactive hypoglycemia* Horm. Meatb. Res. 1981, 13? 646–647

CHILES R. — *Excessive serum insulin response to oral glucose in obesity and mild diabetes* Diabetes 1970, 19, 158

CRAPO P.A. — *The effects of oral fructose, sucrose and glucose in subjects with reactive hypoglycemia* Diabetes care 1982, 5, 512–517

DORNER M. — *Les hypoglycémies fonctionelles* Rev. Prat. 1972, 22, 25, 3427–3446

FAJANS S.S. — *Fasting hypoglycemia in adults* New Engl. J. Med. 1976, 294, 766–772

FARRYKANT M. — *The problem of fonctional hyperinsulinism or fonctional hypoglycemia attributed to nervous causes* Metabolism 1971, 20, 6, 428–434

FIELD J.B. — *Studies on the mechanisms of ethanol induced hypoglycemia* J. Clin. Inverst. 1963, 42, 497–506

FREINKEL N. — *Alcohol hypoglycemia* J. Clin. Invest. 1963, 42, 1112–1133

HARRIS S. — *Hyperinsulinism and dysinsulinism* J.A.M.A. 1924, 83, 729–733

HAUTECOUVERTURE M. — *Les hypoglycémies fonctionnelles* Rev. Prat. 1985, 35, 31, 1901–1907

HOFELDT F.D. — *Reactive hypoglycemia* Metab. 1975, 24, 1193–1208

HOFELDT F.D. — *Are abnormalities in insulin secretion responsible for reactive hypoglycemia?* Diabetes 1974, 23, 589–596

JENKINS D.J.A. — *Decrease in post-prandial insulin and glucose concentrations by guar and pectin* Ann. Intem. Med. 1977, 86, 20–23

JOHNSON D.D. — *Reactive hypoglycemia* J.A.M.A. 1980, 243, 1151–1155

JUNG Y. — *Reactive hypoglycemia in women* Diabetes 1971, 20, 428–434

LEFEBVRE P. — *Statement on post-prandial hypoglycemia* Diabetes cara 1988, 11, 439–440

LEFEBVRE P. — *Le syndrome d'hypoglycémie réactionnelle, mythe ou réalité?* Journées Annuelles de l'Hôtel-Dieu 1983, 111–118

LEICHTER S.B. — *Alimentary hypoglycemia: a new appraisal* Amer. J. Nutr. 1979, 32, 2104–2114

LEV-RAN A.   *The diagnosis of post-prandial hypoglycemia* Diabetes 1981, 30, 996–999

LUBETZKI J.   *Physiopathologie des hypoglycémies* Rev. Prat. 1972, 22, 25, 3331–3347

LUYCKY A.S.   *Plasma insulin in reactive hypoglycemia* Diabetes 1971, 20, 435–442

MONNIER L.H.   *Restored synergistic entero-hormonal response after addition of dietary fiber to patients with impaired glucose tolerance and reactive hypoglycemia* Diab. Metab. 1982, 8, 217–222

O'KEEFE S.J.D.   *Lunch time gin and tonic: a cause of reactive hypoglycemia* Lancet 1977, 1, June 18, 1286–1288

PERRAULT M.   *Le régime de fond des hypoglycémies fonctionnelles de l'adulte* Rev. Prat. 1963, 13, 4025–4030

SENG G.   *Mécanismes et conséquences des hypoglycemies* Rev. Prat. 1985, 35, 31, 1859–1866

SERVICE J.F.   *Hypoglycemia and the post-prandial syndrome* New Engl. J. Med. 1989, 321, 1472

SUSSMAN K.E.   *Plasma insulin levels during reactive hypoglycemia* Diabetes 1966, 15, 1–14

TAMBURRANO G.   *Increased insulin sensitivity in patients with idiopathic reactive hypoglycemia* J. Clin. Endocr. Metab. 1989, 69, 885

TAYLOR S.I.   *Hypoglycemia associated with antibodies to the insulin receptor.* New Engl. J. Med. 1982, 307, 1422–1426

YALOW R.S.   *Dynamics of insulin secretion in hypoglycemia* Diabetes 1965, 14, 341–350

Technical Appendix 2

Part Two

by
Professor Attilio Giacosa
*Head of Nutrition at the National
Cancer Institute (Genoa, Italy)*

Biography

Professor Attilio Giacosa was born in Neive, Italy in 1948. He graduated in 1973 from the University of Turin, where he wrote his experimental thesis on the radio-immunological determination of gastrin in humans.

After spending two years in the Nutritional and Intestinal Unit at the General Hospital in Birmingham (England), he became a specialist in diseases of the digestive tract and digestive endoscopy.

From 1976, he collaborated with the Gastroenterology Department at the San Martino Hospital in Genoa, working in the field of digestive endoscopy and particularly clinical trials. He then went on to become a specialist in the science on nutrition at the University of Milan.

His studies are currently concentrated on the correlation between nutrition and cancer, where his research is based on an experimental, epidemiological and clinical approach.

Professor Giacosa is a member of several medical societies, director of the unit on clinical nutrition at the National Institute for Cancer Research in Genoa and scientific coordinator of all European Research for the ECP (European Organisation for Cooperation in Cancer Prevention Studies).

In addition, his scientific activity is described in 270 papers and six monographs.

Clinical Utilisation of Dietetic Fibers

In recent years, dietary habits in the industrialised countries have led to the overconsumption of meats, fats, dairy products and breads made with highly refined flour (to the detriment of dietary fiber content). Burkitt has shown that these new dietary habits favor many of today's illnesses (cardiovascular diseases and intestinal disorders).

The recent studies by Del 'Toma (1987) proved that meals rich in fiber can help control dysfunctions of carbohydrate and fat metabolisms and contribute to weight-loss. One of the most important characteristics of the diverse dietary fibers is their degree of solubility in water:

– insoluble fibers (cellulose, hemicellulose, lignin) absorb water, increase the weight and volume of the bowels and reduce the risks of diseases related to intestinal transit, such as diverticulosis and colic cancers.

– soluble fibers (pectin, gum, mucilage) swell and form viscous solutions or gels in the digestive tube. This contributes to a certain feeling of fullness and reduces the intestinal absorption of carbohydrates and lipids.

Among these fibers, glucomannane and the Beta vulgaris fiber are the most useful:

The Beta vulgaris fiber:

These fibers are obtained from beets which contain 25% soluble fibers (pectin) and 75% insoluble fibers (cellulose 31%; hemicellulose 4.5%, lignin 2.5%). Professor Giacosa has shown their effectiveness against chronic constipation. In fact, there is only a 3.8% failure rate after one month of treatment. This result is obtained through the regulation of the bowel movement activity and the increase of the fecal volume. Fecal consistance is also modified, since the feces are soft in 69.3% of the cases.

The presence of the soluble fibers means that beet fibers may also be prescribed for carbohydrate and fat metabolism problems. Beet fibers represent 77.82% of the total dry weight of the plant, which is more than the 40% of fibers found in bran.

Glucomannane:

Glucomannane is a derivative of the Amorpho Phallus Konjac plant family, grown in Japan. This fiber expands in water, absorbing 200 times its weight, and forms a viscous and gelatin-like mass. It reduces the absorption of some carbohydrates and lipids (See graphs I and II.) In addition, it has proven to be effective in the treatment of obesity, as shown by the studies by Professor Giacosa (1989). If glucomannane (.14 oz or 4 g per day, taken three times before meals) is added to the diet, the subject loses 10.7 lbs. by the end of the month, whereas 7.26 lbs. are lost by control subjects taking a placebo. However, there is no difference whatsoever if the dose is reduced to 0.07 oz or 2 g per day.

	Average Weight	Weight at end of treatment	Difference
Glucomannane (4 g/day)	185 ± 10.3	174 ± 14.7	− 11
Placebo	183 ± 18.7	176 ± 16.7	− 7

Glucomannane is used today in the various dietary preparations, especially pasta, and together with guar gum. This pasta reduces the post-prandial hyperglycemic peak and considerably diminishes the pancreatic secretion (See graphs III and IV), and is thus useful for the obese and type II diabetics.

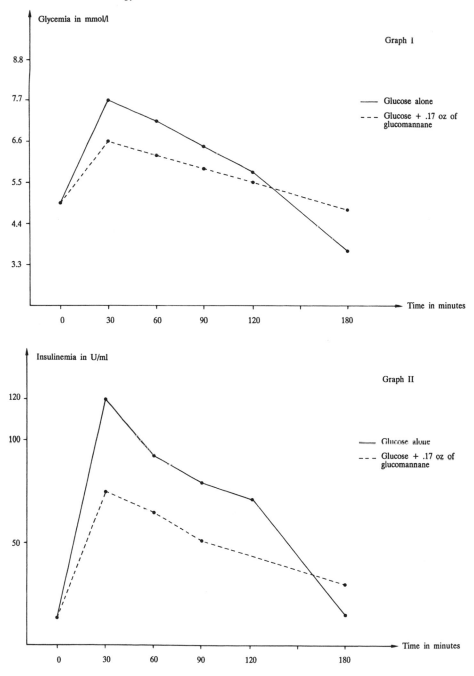

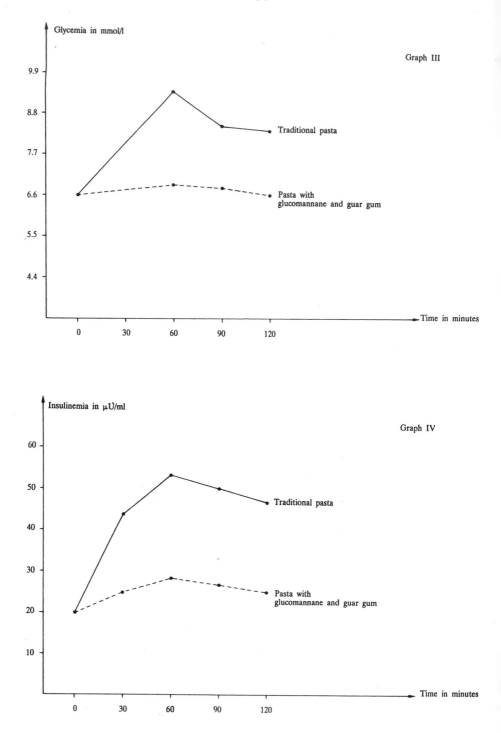